Penology, Justice and Liberty

Are You a Man or a Mouse?

James C. McEleney
Barbara Lavin McEleney

UNIVERSITY PRESS OF AMERICA,® INC.
Lanham • Boulder • New York • Toronto • Oxford

Copyright © 2005 by
University Press of America,® Inc.
4501 Forbes Boulevard
Suite 200
Lanham, Maryland 20706
UPA Acquisitions Department (301) 459-3366

PO Box 317
Oxford
OX2 9RU, UK

Library of Congress Control Number: 2004113583
ISBN 0-7618-2986-5 (clothbound : alk. ppr.)
ISBN 0-7618-2987-3 (paperback : alk. ppr.)

We dedicate this book to our parents who taught us
about justice and fairness, and
to our son, James, that he might live in, and contribute to,
a world of peace and justice and understanding among peoples.

Contents

Acknowledgements

We would like to thank our respective academic institutions, St. Thomas Aquinas College and Marist College for the sabbatical leaves of absence which enabled us to write the rough draft of this manuscript while living in England.

Many people gave encouragement along the way and valuable technical support.

To Dean Margaret Calista, thank you for believing in this work.

To Bill VanOrnum, we thank you for your words of encouragement when they were needed the most and for reading through the entire first draft when you were also busy with your own research and writing.

To Mohamed Tazari and Amity Currie, we thank you for solving the periodic word processing dilemmas.

To Kimberly Albin, we thank you for painstaking checking of several references.

To all our colleagues, neighbors and friends who listened and encouraged, thank you.

To James, who lived with this project for several years and who probably ate more take-out meals than is healthy, a heartfelt thank you for your sense of humor, patience and good will.

Introduction

This book is intended primarily as a discussion of the various theories and practices in the area of penology (what we do, or ought to do, to those convicted of having committed a crime). If we assume that a crime has been committed, that the police have apprehended the criminal, that the criminal has been given a fair trial and that the verdict is guilty, now what are we going to do with the criminal and why? In many ways this is the most puzzling part of the criminal justice system and various answers have been asserted.

PRELIMINARY CONSIDERATIONS

Any sentence imposed by the criminal justice system is, by its very nature, coercive, as it is imposed and inflicted by the power of the state independent of the will of the person sentenced. As such, it involves the loss of liberty and some measure of pain, regardless of its degree of humaneness.

Since we live in a democracy, this sentence is imposed in our name and on our behalf, or, more particularly, as each of us must recognize, it is imposed in my name and on my behalf. The field of penology (or theories of punishment) then is not a mere academic abstract intellectual exercise, though, indeed, it is a complex intellectual field. It is also one that imposes on each of us the moral (or ethical, if you prefer) obligation to examine and justify what we are doing. To inflict pain on another without careful consideration would, indeed, be callous and indistinguishable from the same attitude that we condemn in the criminal. The level of our concern and the quality of the decisions we achieve are measures of our own moral worth and intellectual integrity.

Of course, we are all very concerned about the level of crime in our society and about our own personal safety and that of those we love. Our consciousness and anxiety are prompted and maintained by the news media's constant reporting of the latest horrendous events, such as the Columbine high school massacre in the United States, by the television industry constantly entertaining us with stories of crime detection (factual and fictional), and of the heroics and muscle power of our crime fighters. It pours forth into our living rooms in living color and the gorier the graphics the better. We seem to live in a sea of crime surrounded by bad and dangerous people. As individuals we feel helpless and threatened and buy better locks for our doors. No wonder that we feel that something must be done and done urgently.

But we have also been primed to accept that the something which must be done is the same solution as that which television continuously presents to us: detection, apprehension, trial and presumed imprisonment. Of course, the trial and imprisonment stages are usually omitted and the program ends with apprehension. These later stages are not usually entertaining enough to maintain Nielsen ratings.

On the proactive side, we are busy eliminating the vulnerabilities which permit crime to happen in the first place by installing metal detectors in schools, airports, federal and state buildings, and ubiquitous security television cameras. We encourage greater police efficiency in preventing crime by purchasing new equipment, surveillance of "dangerous" people and organizations, inter-agency sharing of computerized data, weakening of stop and search rules, and so on.

In brief, the solution seems to be to do more of the same: hire more police, catch more criminals, give tougher sentences, and build and fill more prisons, policies which, especially since we declared war on drugs, have been intensifying for over a quarter of a century.

As Gavin Esler noted in his, *The United States of Anger* (1997),

By 1995, the United States had imprisoned 1.6 million adults—the same number of men and women as were then in all branches of the U.S.

military. This number had TRIPLED since 1980 . . . At least another
3.75 million were on probation or parole. (tripled italicized in original).

(Esler, 1997: 113)

There is no question that in the almost thirty years since the riot at
Attica State prison in New York State our prison system has become
more punitive. This has reflected the general mood of the country since
the era of Reaganomics, that spending for causes perceived as liberal,
such as rehabilitation for criminal offenders, is neither cost effective
nor morally necessary. And the number of the incarcerated continues
to escalate throughout the United States. Between 1997 and 1998, five
states (Mississippi, North Dakota, Wisconsin, Vermont and Oregon) all
experienced more than an 11% increase in their prison populations.
Mississippi was among the highest at 16.7% (Haberman, 2000:7). Between 1974 and 2000, the number of state and federal prisons increased from 592 to 1,023, with the result that in 2004, some counties
had thirty percent of their residents behind bars (Butterfield, 2004:
A19).

Worse still, these policies have a disproportionate impact on minorities. Over a quarter of all African American males between the
ages of 18 and 30 are under the control of the criminal justice system,
awaiting trial, in prison or on parole. In Baltimore, Maryland, this figure has reached 50%. According to The Sentencing Project, in 1996,
the incarceration rate for African Americans was 7.66 times greater
than that of whites, up from 6.88 times in 1988 (Thomas, 1997:A:03).
And, since inmates are barred from voting in most of the United States,
another consequence of this is the disenfranchisement of many African
Americans. As the November 2004 Presidential election approached,
4.7 million Americans would not be permitted to vote because they
were either in prison or had felony convictions. Of these, 1.4 million
were African American men. Thirteen percent of African American
men are disenfranchised, some permanently, "a rate seven times the
national average" (Fellner and Mauer, 1998, 2004: 1).

And there are other political consequences of incarceration policies.
In the state of New York, where most prisons are located in remote
rural, generally Republican, areas, the prison inmates are counted as
residents and their numbers increase the political representation and
allocation of funding to these often economically deprived areas de-

spite the fact that these inmates have no vote. Moreover, since these inmates are disproportionately from the more Democratic urban areas,
their incarceration in rural areas also serves to decrease the political
representation and funding allocated to the urban areas of the state.

One other little examined consequence of the current incarceration
policies in America is the impact of these policies on the prisoners'
families. Frequently they are left without a breadwinner and are unable
to pay essential bills such as rent and electricity. In many states, prisons are located far from their homes and family members must incur
additional expenses and difficulties visiting their loved ones. Few formerly intact family units are able to survive the separation and hard-
ships, a consequence of the lengthy sentences imposed by American
courts. And what of the impact on children visiting family members in
prisons and jails, or the effect on the community in which the prisoners lived? Is the entire community stigmatized, thus contributing to
discrimination even against the law abiding?

What has happened to the focus on rehabilitation, which was so popular during the 1950's and 1960's that prisons were renamed correctional facilities, prison guards were renamed correctional officers and
prison wardens became superintendents?

Forty years later, we could not be farther from that image of an "enlightened" penal policy. Prison construction for the 21st century reflects the ideology of security and custody and not rehabilitation. New
prison cells are designed to isolate inmates from one another and from
their custodians. The description that follows is from New York State,
but similar construction can be found in maximum security blocks
throughout the United States. These futuristic cells are designed to
contain inmates twenty-three hours a day with one hour each day of
court mandated outdoor recreation. Each 105 sq. ft. cell contains a
shower and toilet, with an electronically controlled rear door leading to
an enclosed recreation area. Inmates are totally isolated from each
other and from the custodial staff except in very limited circumstances
("Budget OKs", 1998:6 and "System-wide SHU", 1998:14). In situations where the inmate is deemed to be a danger to the staff, specially
prepared meals are arranged in a roll of dough and merely passed
through a slot in the door. Surrounding these prison cells are inner
fences, topped and banked with razor wire, microwave detection systems and an exterior fence again topped and banked with razor wire

("Budget OKs", 1998:6). Inmates in the 21st century will serve sentences, often life sentences if convicted under habitual offender legislation, of virtual solitary confinement.

As we can see, there are diverse, mixed and often conflicting goals given for our penal policies. We are befuddled and confused about what we are trying to achieve (whether retribution, rehabilitation, deterrence or social defense). When we argue about our conflicting viewpoints concerning penal practices, we are often unaware of the taken-for-granted presuppositions and assumptions on which these viewpoints are based. As long as these remain unexamined, we remain confident in our convictions. But when these assumptions are raised for our conscious scrutiny, we may find that our secure mental edifice has been built on quicksand.

Many, if not most, of the current books in the field of criminal justice introduce the reader to its intellectual forefathers by simply presenting what they said, and their arguments for it, in a rather historically a-contextual and uncritical manner, leaving the uninitiated reader to his/her as yet uninformed resources to critique what has been said in an ad hoc, poorly informed way. But this is akin to allowing civilians to wander through an intellectual mine field without benefit of a map or guidelines.

This book is an attempt to understand how we have arrived at these "solutions" to our problem of living with one another. We will explore the various theories of punishment on which these policies are based and the politics of the resulting policies. This book is designed as an introduction to theories of punishment. It will not be exhaustive but hopefully will encourage the reader to further study and reflection.

Chapter One

Are You a Man or a Mouse?

We have been relying on the criminal justice system to keep people safe, to reduce crime and cure criminal offenders of law breaking behavior. But, as the police have recognized, their task is not really to reduce crime but merely to apprehend law-breakers. A law-abiding society is the responsibility of all of us. We must all be engaged in the development of our own character and in helping others to develop theirs so that we can live together in peace and harmony. Therefore, punishment is really a consequence of our failure to solve the problem of how to live with one another in a social context. And perhaps the fact that we even have to devise a punishment system is as much a failure on the part of the law abiding as it is a failure on the part of the law-breaker.

Indeed the problem of our own moral character may be fundamental to our ability to live together in a society, as many writers as diverse as Stark (1976), Tonnies (1963), Durkheim (1951 and 1953), Ortega y Gasset, and Schopenhauer (1893), to name a few, have discussed. Schopenhauer (1893:142), for example, discusses the human problem as similar to that of porcupines on a cold day; separated they freeze, but when they huddle together for warmth, they prick each other with their quills. They thus have to mutually accommodate to minimize pricking and maximize the warmth. We, too, need each other and we must find ways to live together pleasantly, minimizing our mutual antagonisms. Stark, especially, has noted that our social bond is not given by nature as is, for example, that of the cooperative beehive. In discussing our efforts to live together in a mutually pleasant way he notes that civilization is an achievement of man and consists in the restraint and control of our animal impulses, not their free unfolding. In his *The Social Bond*, vol. 1 (1976), he clarifies the crucial but often obscured fact that humans have intelligence rather than instinct. This issue may deserve some development at this point as it relates to the nature vs. nurture debate in the social sciences which has ramifications for our conceptions of ourselves, and our social and political relationships, including our criminal justice policies. Clearly a complete discussion of this debate is beyond the scope of this work. However, an introductory understanding of the gist of this fundamental distinction is necessary for later discussions, because this nature/nurture debate has important ramifications for the punishment theories of retribution, social defense, deterrence and the punishment/treatment theory of rehabilitation.

The nature approach to the study of man basically claims that:

1) the universe is deterministic and follows unavoidable sequences of cause and effect. In essence, there is simply no such thing as free will (voluntarism) anywhere in the universe. It simply does not exist. Period.
2) man is just another part of this deterministic universe and he, too, is caused to do all that he does by forces or mechanisms of nature, which we should seek to discover. Even man's thinking is a product of nature. Man simply has no "free will."
3) explanations even of human events are to be in terms of efficient causality, showing which quantifiable causes lead to which quantifiable effects.
4) just as a knowledge of the natural sciences enables us to design and control the physical world, so, too, can a knowledge of the science of man and society enable us to manipulate and control man himself, ostensibly for his own good.

Indeed, we do exist in nature and so submit to nature's laws as far as our material parts are concerned. No one denies that our physical bodies are subject to laws of chemistry, physics, and biology. I cannot fly like a bird nor eat grass like a cow. But this is not what we are talking about when we refer to the nature approach to the study of man. The real question is whether or not our thinking, our ideas, are caused by forces or mechanisms of nature and are thus a mere by-product of nature, an epiphenomenon, a mere illusion. For, on analysis, as we shall see, this is the central claim of the nature approach to the study of man in the earliest version of it.

However, if one claims that our thinking is a mere epiphenomenon, a mere illusion, then the same would have to be said of the thinking of the scientists making such a claim. Their thought processes would also have to be an epiphenomenon, caused and therefore not what is generally known as thinking. Thus, their thinking has no real meaning, no validity. Their claim reduces itself to meaninglessness akin to the Epimenides dilemma, a simplified version of which is the statement, "I always lie." On analysis no sense can be made of such a statement. Logically, the nature approach claim reduces itself to "all thinking is an illusion with no real meaning" and the same applies to this claim. It is a statement that cannot be made- thus, intellectual nihilism.

Interestingly, scientists often put themselves outside this frame. Thus, the proponents of the scientific approach believe they have real knowledge while the rest of us are merely puppets of nature. For biologists, the thinking mechanism is reduced to biological forces of nature; for psychologists, like Freud, it is the unconscious forces of the id and the superego; for behaviorists like Skinner and others, it is the environment reduced to stimulus response which produces thought.

While the exact origins of this nature approach might be endlessly debated, as an introduction to its development and influence on modern thought, it may be useful to examine some of the events and conflicts in the time of Galileo (1564–1642).

When Galileo, agreeing with Copernicus, began to teach that the earth moves, rotating on its axis daily and traveling around the sun each year, this was the cause of much consternation among the ordinary people. The common view at that time was that the earth was the center of the universe and that the heavens (sun, moon, stars, and planets) revolved around the earth. This, of course, meant that the earth was the most important part of the universe and, since man was the most important thing on earth, man was the most important thing in the universe.

However, if, as Galileo taught, the earth moves, then the earth loses its place of central importance in the great scheme of things and man himself is reduced to being an insignificant passenger-spectator, unimportant and peripheral. European man's self confidence had already recently been shaken by reports from the voyages of discovery of other civilizations with more advanced mathematics, legal systems, and religions other than Christianity. This new claim of Galileo's, in a sense, shook the very ground from under their feet. Its implications were truly disorienting and unacceptable, thus they argued against it as being counter to common sense and everyday experience. One could watch the sun travel across the sky while sitting still and one's surroundings being motionless. The very evidence of one's senses verified for them that the earth did not move.

But Galileo knew that it did. How did he know? For generations the locations of the planets (wanderers) had been recorded as they traveled among the fixed stars. Generations of astronomers had spent lifetimes trying to explain the mechanics of the heavens with various combinations of spheres rolling on other spheres with planets affixed to them, each sphere rolling on another sphere being called an epicycle (Bronowski and Mazlish, 1960). This trial and error method of predicting the location of a planet on a given night was cumbersome and time consuming. As an example of its complexity, it took 87 epicycles to predict the pathway of Mars, for Venus, it took 96.

And even that did not correlate Mars to Venus except indirectly. Even when Copernicus had made the imaginative leap of observing the universe as if he were standing on the face of the sun and assuming the earth revolving around it, the problem of epicycles did not completely disappear. Since the orbits of the planets, as we now know, are elliptical, it still took 37 epicycles to force Mars into a circular path. But 37 epicycles are much simpler than 87! Galileo took the records of the varying locations of the planets, analyzed them mathematically using Copernicus' conceptual scheme, and agreed with Copernicus that this was evidence that the earth revolved around the sun. This together with his observations of the four moons in complex orbit around Jupiter convinced him of that fact. This led Galileo to state that those who opposed his views were deceived by their deficient senses, which convinced them that the sun did the moving.

I think that these tastes, colors, odors etc . . . are nothing else than mere names, but hold their residence solely in the sensitive body; so that if the animal were removed, every such quality would be abolished and annihilated.

(Quoted in Matson, 1966:4)

And we would be left with the real truth of the universe, that matter simply follows laws of motion. So the experience of life as it is lived and felt is reduced to the realm of error and irrelevancy while only the abstract, impersonal and real truth of mechanical nature is of consequence. It is important to grasp the implications of what is being said here. On one hand it is a claim about the superiority of scientific method (quantifiable observations, mathematical analysis) as a way of knowing the real truth as opposed to the commonsensical view of things. But it is also the beginning of the division of people into two categories: the knowers being those who have arrived at the truth using scientific method and the non-knowers being all others who are assumed to have been led astray by non- scientific method.

To some, it seemed that Galileo's claim that the earth moved contradicted the descriptions in the Bible and hence undermined religion. As early as 1615, he had asserted the truth of science over the truth of religion

> I conceive that, concerning natural effects, that which either sensible experience sets before our eyes or necessary demonstrations do prove unto us, ought not, upon any account, to be called into question, much less condemned upon the testimony of texts of scripture . . .
> (Quoted in Bronowski and Mazlish, 1960:125)

Galileo was summoned to the Vatican in 1633 and coerced to recant under threat of being burned as a heretic. Subsequently, he was prohibited from teaching publicly that the earth moves and was put under house arrest near Florence until his death in 1642. Here, he was visited by his admirers from distant parts of Europe, among them Francis Bacon and John Milton from England, who were enthralled by this new and infallible method of finding the truth. What we would now call the scientific method was then called positive philosophy as opposed to the earlier scholastic philosophy of Aristotle and Aquinas. Henceforth, theology and philosophy which dealt with unmeasurable unobservables were to be categorized as "idle speculation", essentially a waste of time.

Nevertheless, science can deal only with what is, that is, with empirically demonstrable relations between observable phenomena and thus is merely descriptive. No amount of mere description of what is can ever tell us what we ought to do. The epistemological rules of science, rules limiting acceptable (because supposedly "proved") truth to a description of observables, simply precludes discussion of normative standards. These are relegated to the realm of the unobservable, and hence unprovable realm of mere value judgments, mere personal preferences having no scientific validity. Moral standards, then, are assumed to be scientifically non-discussable and irrelevant. We can no longer ask questions like "what is justice?"

Since the scientific method was the only way of arriving at the real truth about anything, that method had to be employed in studying everything, even in the study of man himself. But, since science can deal only with deterministic, measurable cause and measurable effect sequences, man had to be reduced to being just another causally determined part of the universe, and conceptions of free will or human responsibility had to be banished from existence or consideration. In seventeenth century Holland, Spinoza railed against the advocates of free will in declaring that

> Most writers on the emotions and on human conduct . . . seem to be treating rather of matters outside nature than of natural phenomena following nature's general laws. They appear to conceive man to be situated in nature as a kingdom within a kingdom; for they believe he disturbs rather than follows nature's order.
>
> (Quoted in Matson, 1966:8)

For his part, Spinoza declared

> I shall consider human actions and desires in exactly the same manner as though I were concerned with lines, planes and solids.
>
> (Quoted in Matson,1966:8)

This view of man as being a purely passive object, as nature bound as any inanimate object in a mechanical universe, became the generally accepted view of the enthusiasts of science over time and was clearly expressed by some of the French *philosophes* many generations later. For example, La Mettrie is quoted as saying

> Let us conclude boldly then that man is a machine and that there is only one substance, differently modified, in the whole world. What will all the weak reeds of divinity, metaphysic, and nonsense of the schools,

avail against this firm and solid oak? . . . If we assume the least principle of motion, then animated bodies will have all they require in order
to move, to feel, to think, to repent, and in short to conduct themselves
physically and, which is dependent on this, morally.

(Quoted in Matson, 1966:13–14)

Holbach, too, accepted this deterministic view of man as a being
rooted in nature.

He exists in nature. He is submitted to her laws. He cannot deliver himself from them. . . . The universe, that vast assemblage of everything that
exists, presents only matter and motion: the whole offers to our con-
templation nothing but an immense, an uninterrupted succession of
causes and effects.

(Quoted in Randall, 1940:274)

Descartes, also, epitomized this faith in science, claiming we should
"concern ourselves only with those matters which can be known with
certainty," and the mathematical sciences provide the appropriate norm
for that certitude. Thus, in *Rules for the Direction of the Mind (1628)*,
Descartes states

. . . in our search for the direct road towards truth, we should busy ourselves with no object about which we cannot attain a certitude equal to
that of the demonstrations of Arithmetic and Geometry.

(Descartes, (1628) 1955:5)

With Newton the faith in the scientific method became absolute.
When Isaac Newton explained the workings of the whole universe
in terms of laws of motion and universal centripetal gravitation
which explained equally the motions of the planets, why the moon
did not fall, and how an apple fell on earth, it seemed that science
had totally explained how the universe worked. It seemed like Newton had achieved absolute knowledge once and for all. It was
LaPlace who remarked

that Newton was not only the greatest genius that ever had existed, but
also the most fortunate; inasmuch as there is but one universe, and it can
therefore happen to one man in the world's history to be the interpreter
of its laws.

(Quoted in Burtt, 1924:18)

The knowledge that science gave was presumed to be objective, absolute and cumulative. It was presumed to be objective in the sense that they thought that facts spoke for themselves, you simply had to observe something and to analyze what you had observed mathematically and the truth would be self-evident. They assumed it to be absolute knowledge in the sense that once a truth had been discovered, it was the final, ultimate and complete truth about the thing. It was assumed to be cumulative in the sense that they believed that science would eventually find the true answer to absolutely everything. It was merely a matter of piling truth upon truth upon truth until absolutely everything was explained.

This uncritical acceptance of the exclusive validity of scientific method in achieving the ultimate truth was common, and still pervades much of our thinking today. It was simply assumed that there could be a science of everything, including a science of man and society.

However, we now know that scientific revolutions occur in which paradigms of the former normal science are abandoned and are replaced by totally new conceptions and explanations of reality. For example, the Genesis picture of the universe gives way to the Ptolemaic system of the universe, which gives way to the Copernican-Newtonian conception of the universe, which gives way to Einsteinian relativity, which is currently moving towards post-Einsteinian paradigms. Each of these involves the creation of a new concept of reality, and its corresponding new explanations of its workings. The fact that scientific revolutions occur is evidence that facts do not speak for themselves and that science itself is only man interpreting reality, making an understanding of his world. It is evidence that man is the interpreter of his world. The very nature of science shows that the reality of man is different from that imposed by mere nature. He creates the meaning of things, which is the claim of the nurture approach. But this last insight has become available only recently to philosophers of science.

Most people, even those involved in the sciences of man and society, have unconsciously or uncritically accepted the assumptions of the nature approach as we have outlined it. It saturates the social sciences from the time of Galileo until today.

As we wend our way through the various theories and policies of punishment, the influence of this thinking will become apparent. This puppet on the strings of nature version of man conduces to the assumption that the pathetic puppet is to be controlled or manipulated for his own good, the benevolence of the puppeteers being unquestionable.

Thus, for example, Comte, one of the founding fathers of Sociology, thought he could create a "Social Physics," a science of society emulating Newton's accomplishments in the material (physical) world and optimistically titled one of his early essays, "The Plan of the Scientific Operations Necessary for Reorganizing Society." This newly founded science was to enable sociology to become the queen of the sciences and the sociologists to become the high priests of society, benevolently and scientifically directing its future. For Comte, this recognition that

> history is as spontaneously law-governed as astronomy and chemistry . . .
> led to an altogether different, new, and 'scientific' conception of politics.
> (Sragens, 1981:132)

This science of man was not to remain an impotent theoretical abstraction. Its entire purpose was expressed in Comte's own words: "*Savoir pour prevoir, prevoir pour pouvoir.*" To know to foresee, to foresee in order to do something about it. For Comte,

> the 'social physicist' first 'observes' the previous course of history, finding in it the regular and determinate laws of succession that govern it. On the basis of this knowledge, he can then obtain a 'scientific prevision' of social phenomena 'within the limits of exactness compatible with their higher complexity'. . . . This . . . provides then 'the fundamental datum and positive starting point of general practical politics' in the scientific mode.
> (Quoted in Sragens, 1981:133)

Thus, Comte's presumed status as a scientist confers on Comte, at least in his own estimation, the right to rule and usurp the powers that we would confer and limit by democratic elections. His right to decide our fate becomes absolute and unlimited by virtue of Comte's infallible, omnipotent, scientific status.

For Comte, there was a law of nature that caused the stages of thought in history. "Because the course of history is predetermined, no one can alter its basic end" (Sragens, 1981:133). The initial stage was that of theology where explanations were rooted in superstition or religion. The second stage was metaphysical where explanations and discussions were philosophical (for example, natural law theory or scholastic philosophy). The third stage was scientific, and only in this stage can we understand that there is a scientific cause and effect sequence to everything. It is only at this stage where a science of man and society can be developed, thus giving man, or Comte, the ability to understand scientifically the natural historical progress of man and society and the ability and the right to direct it. Interestingly, Comte gives no specific content to the science of society that would be the result.

For Comte, history is governed by the "workings of natural laws" (Spragens, 1981:132).

> Because history is governed by natural laws, it proceeds on its course essentially 'independent of the human will'. Historical events are the result of 'necessary' rather than accidental' causes. History follows a 'determined and invariable course' and is characterized by 'unavoidable transitions.'
>
> (Quoted in Spragens, 1981:132)

The above view about man gives rise to what Spragens calls the logic of domination and the technocratic political agenda (Spragens, 1981). Since the knowers, the possessors of the infallible scientific method which arrives at the "real" truth, believe they can discover the forces and mechanisms of nature at work in steering man and society in whatever direction, they begin to assume that this knowledge must be put to "good" use in controlling human behavior and in creating the "good" society as decided by them. Just as the knowledge of the laws of nature governing the material world can be used constructively, that is, to design an engine with the required motive power or brakes with required stopping power, so, too, could the laws of nature governing the world of man and society be used scientifically to produce desired outcomes.

That the desirability of such outcomes is itself a value judgment outside the scope of supposedly value neutral science and is based on the particular political ideology of the individual theorist seems to have eluded consideration, hidden from view in the cloak of science.

Thus Hobbes could deduce that man in the state of nature (before he lived in societies) was by nature selfish and brutish by logically abstracting from him all the civilized qualities. The natural conditions would then be a state of war "of every man against every other man," each acting selfishly, distrusting and fearing each other, with "the life of man (being) solitary, poor, nasty, brutish, and short" (Hobbes, (1651) 1960:82).

Starting from this atomistic view of isolated brutish individuals, how could society develop? Hobbes' solution, put forth in his book titled, *The Leviathan* (1651), is that they had to create a Leviathan, a powerful sovereign or state to rule over them with absolute authority to tell them what to do, and, by force and fear, restrain each predatory individual from victimizing the other.

Accordingly, the power of the sovereign (or the state) had to be absolute power, and the duty of its subjects was but to obey, or suffer the wrathful vengeance of the Leviathan. Order in society, then, comes from above, from those wielding the power and authority of the state, and is imposed on us only by our fear of punishment. Without such fear we would be incapable of living peaceably with each other for we are by nature amoral.

> To this war of every man, against every man, this also is consequent; that nothing can be unjust. The notions of right and wrong, justice and injustice have there no place. Where there is no common power, there is no law: where no law, no injustice.
>
> (Hobbes, (1651) 1960:83)

It is clear that this is an argument proposing and legitimizing a political agenda because it proposes the unfettered power of the state and the docile obedience of its subjects together with criminal justice policies based on deterrence. This is the law and order approach as crudely conceived—tough laws and harsh penalties. Given our current consciousness of crime levels and daily fare of the media, it is easy to agree with such simplistic and unanalyzed solutions as these. And conjoined with our interpersonal relations of individual competitiveness with little or no regard or responsibility for each other's quality of life, (the modern version of each against all), we do live in an atmosphere of mutual mistrust, a sort of social isolation, of "keep your guard up and watch your back."

This mutual mistrust and the proposed "get tough" solutions to crime are mutually reinforcing and lead to crime control as a central emphasis of sound-bite politicians and of government. What is ignored are other more positively constructive purposes and policies to which governments might aspire in ameliorating the quality of life and enabling the achievement of the social aspirations of the citizenry — issues in employment, health, education and the facilitation of the human potentials of each person.

But the problem of the Hobbesian dilemma is already well known. If, as Hobbes claims, man is by nature amoral, then this would also have to be true of the Leviathan—he or they would have to be by nature amoral also. In which case, the Leviathan would be as corrupt as the rest of us. We would simply end up being persecuted and exploited by a powerful crook.

While this unavoidable logic discloses the fallacy in the Hobbesian solution to the problem of creating and maintaining order in a society, the issue is of more than abstract intellectual interest. The past century has provided us with actual governments which have abused their power and acted atrociously. Even presidents of the United States have been of less than irreproachable character, though those selected as such may depend on one's particular party affiliation. Clearly, the citizens of any nation or state have a practical interest in limiting the power which their government may exercise over them.

One might speculate to what degree Hobbes' Leviathan solution to the problem of order was influenced by three factors: first, his admiration for the logic of proof in geometry which led him to his scientific rationalism, the faith that everything could be logically deduced; second, his reduction of the universe, including man, to nothing but matter totally explainable eventually by the laws of matter in motion. "Thus, mind will be nothing, but the motions in certain parts of an organic body" (Quoted in Matson 1966:7).

As Bronowski and Mazlish put it,

> In a world composed of bodies in motion, what is man? He, too, Hobbes believed, was merely a body or, better, a machine, in motion.
> (Bronowski and Mazlish, 1960:197)

The third factor was Hobbes' place in the social structure of his time. He was tutor to Lord Cavendish's family, and the disruptions caused by the Puritan Revolt threatened the established order on which his life style depended. An all-powerful Leviathan firmly maintaining the traditional order would preserve that life style and would be seen as utterly non-threatening to Hobbes.

Karl Marx, likewise, claimed to have a science of society. But, for Marx, the explanatory cause lay in the evolutionary progress of the relations of production, that is, in the means of producing the necessities of life, and the relation of people to those means, and to each other based on their relations to the means. Thus, Marx understood there to be what he called six stages of history: hunter gatherer, slave society, feudalism, industrial capitalism, socialism and communism, each automatically evolving into the other in a necessary and unavoidable sequence. Marx would have claimed that all of the ideas of a particular time were caused by these relations of production—hence these ideas were mere epiphenomena. But, since Marx the scientist, similar to Comte, had scientific understanding of this law of progress, he could hasten it towards its inevitable outcome. All that needed to be done was to transform the relations of production, and the false consciousness, the erroneous epiphenomenal ideas of the currently unacceptable stage, would simply evaporate and dissolve into nothingness.

As this form of thinking has already been put into practice by rulers like Lenin, now we have a practical history where we can see its political consequences carried to its extreme logical conclusion. Lenin claimed to have the science of the progress of human history, true knowledge, real thinking, while those who disagreed with him were assumed to be in a state of false consciousness in which their ideas were merely the product of natural causes. This false consciousness was not to be discussed nor argued with. Those afflicted were not to be shown the error of their ways as one might do in a disagreement between equals when one would try to convince the other by bringing new evidence into consideration or logically showing the errors in his understanding. The benevolent dictator simply transforms these ideas by transforming living conditions.

> He (Lenin) readily admits that the workers of the world do not develop 'socialist consciousness' on their own: . . . (only) those enlightened few, the vanguard, themselves, members of the bourgeois intelligentsia, know the truth . . . It is they who are entitled, indeed obligated, to engage in a 'fierce struggle against spontaneity', to 'divert the working-class movement' from its own goals and 'bring it under the wing of revolutionary Social-Democracy.
>
> (Spragens, 1981:147)

One could continue to trace the development of this view about the nature of man through all the developments of the natural sciences, psychological, behavioral sciences and social and political sciences, and to show its current heirs and adherents. The literature in this area is vast and crucial reading. [Some authors well worth reading are Spragens, (1981), Matson, (1966) and Jaki, (1978)]. Moreover, there has been a tendency for the nature approach concept of man to undergo changes in the specifics of its explanation as the natural sciences have developed or expanded in the areas of biology, physiology, theories of evolution etc. (Pinker, 2002). We will be returning to this issue later when we discuss the varieties of theories of punishment in their historical development.

But, we hasten to note and crucially emphasize, this reduction of the thinking of man to the status of mere epiphenomena produced by material causes subverts the image of man necessary to undergird democracy, which is based on reasonable discussion between individuals presumed to equally share the human faculties of intelligence and reason.

Let us contrast to this deterministic view of man the opposing view of the nurture approach. The nurture approach claims that man has intelligence, that he interprets (not translates) reality, and decides what he wants out of it based on his understanding. In essence, he chooses the consequence that he desires. Thus, he is responsible for his decisions and what he does. It would claim that each individual human being is equal in this regard, namely, that we are the kind of thing (being) that creates the meaning of the world to us. It might be noted in passing that one of the most fundamental questions human beings have to solve is how we interpret what we are in each other's estimation, in other words, what we mean to each other. If I consider you to be stew meat, I put you in a pot and eat you. If I consider you to be an equal interpreter of reality, sharing the same humanity as I, then, in deciding how we will live together, we may negotiate with each other (as equals) what rights we will give each other and what duties we expect from each other. It is clear that this particular ontological definition of man is the foundation stone on which are built any conceptions of democracy. It is central to the U.S. Constitution and the Bill of Rights.

Explanations of human doings in the nurture approach would have to take into consideration the interpretation of reality by those involved and why they have chosen the particular course of action to achieve their particular desired consequences. This type of explanation is fundamentally different from efficient causality, the cause/effect explanation of the nature approach. It has been rather unfortunately titled "final causality" explanation. A final causality explanation explains in terms of human purposes or intentions. It is the goal that one wants to achieve that explains what one is doing or, as it is philosophically stated, it is the means/ends relationship. The end or goal in the future to be achieved explains the means being taken to achieve it. For example, I came to work today so that I may get my paycheck next week. The purposes of studying man from this viewpoint is not a quest for control of other people but to enable their human liberation, to maximize their human freedom by giving them all the necessary information from which to make adequate decisions.

Our human experience convinces each of us that our thinking is our thinking, an activity in which we engage, and our initial reaction to having it dismissed by the omniscient scientist as an irrelevant by product of mere natural forces is one of incredulity bordering on anger. But how we feel about it is not by itself sufficient to refute the claims of the adherents of the nature approach. We must therefore cite some evidence for the validity of the nurture approach as we have defined it.

In our discussion of the nature approach, we have already talked about the fact that scientific revolutions occur in which the accepted explanation (paradigm) confronts anomalies over time, which anomalies are either squeezed into the framework of the accepted science or are simply ignored for a while. Eventually however, some scientists create a brand new explanation, which accounts for both the facts explained by the earlier normal science and for its anomalies. This new explanation replaces the older explanation. Eventually the new explanation becomes the accepted answer and we relax into thinking that we finally know the answer. But then new anomalies occur and the above process begins anew (Kuhn, 1962).

As we noted, this shows that facts do not speak for themselves and that the accepted scientific answer is only the best explanation that we have been able to create for a time. It shows that science itself is really only a product of human (creativity) ingenuity in creating explanations or interpretations of reality. The fact that scientific revolutions occur is in itself evidence for rejecting the assumptions of the adherents of the nature approach in their explanation of human thought.

Indeed, the adherents of the nature approach are faced with two choices. The first, and only one consistent with their claims, is that their own thinking is also caused by forces or mechanisms of nature and as such is an irrelevant epiphenomenon. But this would mean that their claims are devoid of any claim to validity.

The other alternative is to claim exemption from the condition of the rest of humanity and put oneself on a higher ontological status as one whose thinking is really thinking and not an epiphenomenon. It appears that most of those who are willing to apply the nature approach to the study of others have uncritically taken this self-contradictory step. But, as a matter of consistency, we would claim that what is sauce for the goose. . . .

In brief, to be consistent, the nature approach to the study of man dissolves into intellectual nihilism.

On a more empirical level, the evidence for taking the nurture approach to the study of man involves the distinction between man and the rest of the animal kingdom. This involves the distinction between instinct and intelligence or, to put it another way, the question of man's relationship to his bodily equipment. Again, the literature in this particular area is vast and we propose to give only a skeletal outline as a brief introduction to this important question. [See also, Jaki, (1978); Schumacher, (1977); Becker, (1973); Stark, (1976)].

In brief, the argument runs as follows, animals operate through instinct while humans operate through intelligence. By instinct we mean inborn patterns of behavior which enable the organism to deal with a specific external environment. The most obvious example might be the spider, which, on hatching from its egg, finds itself the right kind of corner and proceeds to spin the web appropriate to its own species. In essence, the spider is a born web-spinner. Immediately it might be objected that we have chosen an example whose instinctive behavior is evident and that the behaviors of some animals appear to be learned. For example, some birds, such as seagulls, will not build nests until they have seen other birds building nests. But as Stark points out, this can be explained by a complex of maturation (the bird has reached the appropriate age), and the mechanisms of stimulus-response (Stark, 1976).

More recent obfuscations of the distinction between animals and humans involve the claim by some scientists that they have taught some primates to talk. This is a rather amazing development insofar as the nature adherents are busy reducing man to the status of mere animal while simultaneously anthropomorphizing animals and according them human abilities. At least, to their credit, many of their fellow scientists claim that this apparent language ability may be explained by the mechanisms of behavior modification about which more will be discussed later. Here we would agree with Noam Chomsky, who considers it as unlikely that apes can talk as it is that there is a species of flightless birds on some island waiting for us to teach them how to fly.

Chomsky's argument is a more modern version of such very ancient axioms as

Natura semper agit per vias brevissimas; Natura nihil facit frustra; Natura neque redundat in superfluis, neque deficit in necessariis.
                                                        (Burtt, 1924:26–27)

Translation: nature does nothing in vain, nor does nature give potentialities that are not actualized. In short, nature does not provide faculties which remain unused. However, fortunately, as Anthony Giddens notes, most people already agree that the animal kingdom operates instinctively, that is, according to the definition we have already given of instinct, and that this is true even of the supposedly "more intelligent" animals (Giddens, 1991:11, 41).

Let us think for a moment about what "being governed by instinct" implies. If we take for example, the case of the spider, it is obvious that its way of living out into the world, its "lifestyle", evolved with the organism and has remained the same for millions of years,- spinning webs and catching flies. Such lifestyles can only change at the glacially slow pace of biological evolution. The spider is not free to say, "sitting here in this corner is boring, I think I'll go and become an entertainer in Las Vegas or get into real estate in Florida." The spider is simply a born web-spinner and catcher of flies. He knows what the world is and what life is about for a spider. In a sense, he has absolute truth. For a spider, the world has a fixed or by-nature-given meaning and he does not have to go to school or read this book. He, his reality and his lifestyle are mere products of nature.

Of course, we might digress at this point to note that the achievement of absolute truth for man would end the potentialities and purposes of human intelligence and we would be in the same position of having fixed forever solutions similar to that of the spider. Beings with the fixed answers of instinct also have a fixed world of interest. When the spider is spinning his web, he is "doing his thing." He is fulfilling his by-nature-given *"raison d'etre."* He has fixed interests and fixed meanings.

The by-nature bound world of the animal is also apparent when we examine the mode of communication in the animal kingdom, namely signals. By a signal, we mean where two events are joined in nature in such a way that where you have one, you have the other, for example, fire and smoke; where you have smoke, you have fire. In the animal kingdom, if I have a female dog in a room, in the course of time she will undergo what biologists call the estrus cycle, in which she becomes a female dog in heat. The body changes its biochemical composition. She has become a very different thing. As this new thing, she emits the odor of a female dog in heat just as an onion smells like an onion. This odor contains pheromones, biological-triggering agents. A male dog in the vicinity, who is "doing his thing," for example, territorial marking, picks up the odor and is transformed by the pheromones into a male dog in heat. He is now a transformed bio-chemical entity whose by-nature given interest is in finding the source of the odor and doing what comes naturally. Thus, if we leave the doors open, he will enthusiastically arrive in the room and each dog will satisfy its own felt needs of the moment.

Let us examine what has occurred. When the female dog became a female dog in heat, she had absolutely no choice in the matter. It was something that happened to her. When she emitted the odor, she could not help it. She simply smelled like what she was. It was not that she wished to relieve the boredom of a dull evening with a sexual fling. The male dog likewise had no choice in the matter. On arrival in the room, he had to do what comes naturally. It would not matter to him whether the female dog was his mother or his sister or the mangiest mutt in town. He could not say, "My, what an ugly dog, I'm out of here." Neither of them is intent on satisfying the needs of the other, but merely in self-gratification. Neither do they ask what he or she will think of them in the morning.

This shows us something about how nature operates and dictates in the animal kingdom. Beings with instinct not only have no choice in the matter, but operate in a self-interested fashion. The same is true of

even those animal behaviors which we anthropomorphize into altru-
ism, behaviors such as maternal instinct. Abundant evidence for this
perspective together with relevant sources may be found in Werner
Stark's, *The Social Bond* vol.1, (1976).

Thus for example, when a bird is feeding a baby bird, it is a matter
of stimulus response. It is really feeding a marking in the baby bird's
throat which says, "Put food here." And, in the absence of such marking, the baby bird will be let starve. Similarly, among the monkeys,
mothering a baby monkey is a selfish relief of the mother's own glan-
dular pressures and bodily sensations. If, as has happened for therapeutic reasons, baby monkey is shaved, even in full view of the mother
monkey, who watches with the semblance of human interest and understanding, the bald baby monkey will be rejected by its mother. If the
mother is given an old coconut mat in its place, she will proceed to lav-
ish her maternal "affections" on the coconut mat, still rejecting her
bald baby. She has no understanding or care for her offspring (Stark,
1976).

Human parenting proceeds from an entirely different source, that is,
from definitions of reality and values, and self-sacrifice as opposed to
selfishness, as we shall see when we discuss human reality. We should
not be deceived by superficial similarities. Strategic differences are
important. If presented with two plates of mushrooms, one of which is
poisoned, it is that fact alone we really need to know, not how apparently similar they are.

As a contrast to the world of animals, we claim that man operates
through intelligence. Intelligence is loosely defined as the ability to
create new solutions to problems; that is, that our answers are not fixed
by nature. Indeed, even the problems themselves are not fixed by nature. It may even be seen as the ability to generate questions. It is almost commonplace in the social sciences to say that humans communicate in symbols rather than signals. Symbols may be defined as a
human convention whereby culturally created "sounds" are agreed
upon to designate a culturally interpreted reality. We say humanly created sounds or culturally created sounds as opposed to those biologically generated, such as a sneeze.

Thus if you took the word "dog," somewhere, sometime, someone
had to create that sound to designate the animal concerned and the rest
of us had to agree to use it to point to the dog. We could have created

any sound, maybe "snert", and, if we had agreed to use it, a dog would now be a "snert." Thus different languages have different sounds for dog, "*chien*", "*perro*", "*madadh*". The sound is not given by nature but is a human creation, a break from the chains of nature, unlike the bark of the German Shepherd. But the word "dog" does not point to an objective reality, it points to a culturally interpreted reality. What does the dog mean to us? Is it food? Is it a status symbol or farm helper? Different societies may have different conceptions of what a dog is.

Again, if someone speaks to us in a language we do not know, we do not understand because we have not agreed to use those sounds to convey those meanings. Any language depends on mutually agreed upon sounds conveying mutually agreed upon meanings, an interpretation of reality, as agreed upon by the language users. Neither the sounds nor the meanings of things are given by nature, but are human creations.

Let us summarize what has been said: for intelligent beings who communicate in symbols the world has no by nature given meaning. We decide what anything means to us. Thus, for example, that which we take for granted as a piece of chalk for writing on blackboards is really only an object in the world for which we have found a use and given it a name, "chalk." The same object, found by a primitive unfamiliar with writing on blackboards, would present to that primitive the initial human question, "What is this"? He might then decide to wear it as a necklace piece (ornament) and to him and his society, it is now a necklace piece (ornament) designated by their cultural sound. Therefore, he has done precisely what we have done. He has invented a meaning for an object in the world and given it a name. Thus, a symbol should not be considered primarily as a mode of communication but as the culturally created meaning of a thing which may subsequently be communicated. What we are showing is that human reality is a culturally created reality. Cultural anthropology provides us with many examples of the diverse interpretations of reality created by different societies.

Given this ability to create the meanings of things, one of the most important things we have to define is human relationships. What is another person to us? And clearly the answer is not given by nature. Not even the most apparently natural relationship of the family is fixed by nature. Where some families are matrilineal, others are patrilineal. In some matrilineal societies, you are only related to your mother's family as in the Trobriand Islanders, and the facts of biology, even where known, are simply discounted as irrelevant.

What another person means to us can have a wide range of extremely different meanings. On the lowest extreme would be the Ifugao—you are merely a head to be taken, an object. For the Ifugao, other persons may be merely a source of trophies, as in the Ifugao practice of killing strangers on sight and taking their heads to mount outside their house to demonstrate their warlike abilities and to intimidate others into leaving them in peace (Hoebel, 1976). Despite the myth of value neutrality, one would hardly consider this an adequate human relationship.

We can, through our thinking, make life as beautiful and fulfilling as possible. Our intelligence enables us to do this. However, we also have the potential through our thinking to make life a hell on earth for others, as in the Holocaust. Here, supposedly scientific theories, asserting the biological superiority of Aryan people were combined with social Darwinistic theories involving notions of progress through survival of the fittest to lay the groundwork for the brutal dehumanization and extermination of those labeled inferior. The fact that we have intelligence gives us the ability to analyze the thinking of the past and to see the consequences of inadequate thinking and to avoid such disasters in the future. As Santayana (1863–1952), Spanish philosopher and poet said, "Those who cannot remember the past are condemned to repeat it."

Biological theories of personality are always fraught with danger in that it is but a short step to asserting the superiority of some and the inferiority of others. Of course, this raises the question of what it means to be a human being. When the American Declaration of Independence (1776) or the United Nations' Universal Declaration of the Rights of Man (1948) declare that all men are created equal, they are recognizing our common characteristic of being an interpreter of reality, a thinking, deciding, and responsible person, and prescind from such biological diversities as race or gender.

If a theory fails to give to others the full dignity of a human being, it is clearly inadequate. Thus, one of the criteria of judging any theory or social system is its consequences for the least privileged and powerful in that system.

This is not to say that this is the only way of criticizing (critiquing) theory. Theories may also be criticized on the basis of their intellectual validity and adequacy to the human condition, avoiding reductionism. When we use the term adequacy, we mean that our understanding of what it means to be a human being must also include a recognition of our ability to rise beyond the level of the animal, to create mutually respectful and civilized human relations. It is our ability to do this, not the level of achievement of it, that makes us human beings. The level to which each of us has achieved it may be the distinguishing characteristic between the criminal and the law abiding.

Let us return to Stark's (1978) statement that civilization is an achievement of men collectively and consists in the limitation and control of our animal impulses, not their free unfolding. Then, briefly consider this achievement. To enable us to live together, we have had to create what might loosely be called the virtues: patience as opposed to impatience, truthfulness as opposed to mendacity, mutual consideration as opposed to gross selfishness.

But the practice of each of these virtues does not come easily. It is only when I am tempted to lose my temper that I must practice the self-restraint of self control. Regardless of how hungry we are when we enter a restaurant, unlike the monkey, who simply takes what he wants from a smaller monkey, we let the elderly enjoy their meal in peace and patiently wait for our own order. The practice of each of these virtues, as Stark notes, does not come easily but requires self control and the limitation of our animal impulses (Stark, 1978). In this sense, civilization is not merely an intellectual achievement but the achievement of our own personal characters through the effort of practicing them. We do not become virtuous or law abiding over night. Character is hard won.

But we might also consider that it is only as we achieve our character that we are of any worth as a human being to anyone else. Consider, if I were a disloyal liar and a cheat, would you want me as a friend? Could I be your true and intimate friend? Would you want me as a spouse or a parent? What would it be like to live in a world of characterless people?

It is only the achievement of character that makes worthwhile human relationships possible; but, we have to consider the reward of achieving our character—the possibility of friendship and intimate relations among friends and family. As noted earlier in the nurture approach, it is our purposes or our intentions, the means-end relationship that explains human doings. When we recognize these rewards of practicing the virtues, we can recognize that it is a goal worth working towards, even as an ideal that may never be perfectly achieved. However, we might also note that as we achieve our character and have a proper respect for the humanity of others, the utilitarian aspects of achieving the social rewards of virtue recede. I am not concerned with achieving the social rewards of virtue but the virtues become part of my own character. Thus, in their studies of the Cheyenne Chief, Llewellyn and Hoebel have noted that the chief's concern for his fellow tribesmen and spirit of goodwill often became reflected in his countenance resulting in a benevolent and kindly expression as he grew old. (Hoebel, 1976: 145) I treat others humanely, simply because it is right.

What we have said so far is a brief explanation of the two different approaches to the study of man—the nature approach and the nurture approach, and the types of explanations of human doings which they seek and the directions in which they point.

To reiterate, the nature approach claims a deterministic universe in which everything is to be explained in efficient causality terms, that is, cause and effect. This denies the possibility of the existence of free will. It claims that all human doings are caused by some forces or mechanisms of nature which it is the scientist's task to discover. Having denied notions of free will, they presume the right to control man ostensibly for his own good. This thinking is clearly found in the deterministic theories of rehabilitation of criminal offenders.

The nurture approach claims that man has intelligence, interprets reality and decides what he wants out of it. Man chooses the consequence he desires. It explains human doings in terms of human intentions or purposes (means-end relationships). It recognizes human aspirations and hopes, life as lived and experienced in the human potential, the consequences of our thinking. This thinking is clearly found in the theory of retribution for criminal offenders.

E.A.Burtt has effectively described the vast differences between these two approaches to man. On the one hand is Newton's view of the cosmos

which saw in man a puny, irrelevant spectator . . . of the vast mathematical system whose regular motions according to mechanical principles constituted the world of nature. The gloriously romantic universe of Dante and Milton, that set no bounds to the imagination of man as it played over space and time, had now been swept away. Space was identified with the realm of geometry, time with the continuity of number. The world that people had thought themselves living in—a world rich with color and sound, redolent with fragrance, filled with gladness, love and beauty, speaking everywhere of purposive harmony and creative ideals— was crowded now into minute corners in the brains of scattered organic beings. The really important world outside was a world hard, cold, colourless, silent and dead; a world of quantity, a world of mathematically computable motions in mechanical regularity.

(Burtt, 1924:236–237)

On the other, man is viewed as

. . . a creator with a mind that soars out to speculate about atoms and infinity, who can place himself imaginatively at a point in space and contemplate bemusedly his own planet. This immense expansion, this dexterity, this ethereality, this self-consciousness gives to man literally the status of a small god in nature. . . .

(Becker, 1973:26)

Chapter Two

Do What You are Told Or Else—
Reflections on Deterrence

Clear thinking requires that we use different words for different concepts. To lump together all the various policies or practices aimed at diminishing the crime rate under the heading of deterrence confuses issues which have very different philosophical and political consequences. For example, it should be clear that to place one's legitimately owned goods in a safe to prevent theft is quite a different issue from Nazi practices of enforcing obedience through threats to kill even the innocent.

VARIATIONS IN THE THEORY OF DETERRENCE

We would make distinctions among the following:

1) the prevention of crime by technical means which do not intrude on the legitimate rights or interests of others, such as bank safes and locks on doors. Insofar as it does not interfere with the legitimate concerns of others, this poses no moral or political issue for analysis, whatever else it is.

   These policies are not generally what theorists mean by deterrence theory even though some theorists seem to include them, confusingly, under the heading of deterrence. Nigel Walker, for example, lumps together dogs, high walls and barbed wire as "on the spot deterrents," noting that punishment need not be a component of deterrence (Walker, 1991:14). We disagree, these are preventives, and

30

should not be considered a part of deterrence theory. We propose that a different term should be used to denote such practices, for example, "legitimate preventives" or some such.

2) the prevention of crime by technical means which may intrude on the civil liberties of others, such as CCTV cameras or the requiring of national identity cards.

These are political issues affecting a population at large and requiring that population to decide what intrusions or loss of liberties they will trade for security, providing no one or no particular group has been singled out for special attention. It is quite possible that the views of those charged with crime control may diverge from the views of the population at large in these matters. But, in the end, it should be a democratic decision. This is quite different from deciding the severity of a sentence based on its efficiency in intimidating would be law-breakers into obedience since such sentences are imposed on one person at a time. At the point where we are inflicting harm or punishment on a particular individual, questions of justice arise. While CCTV cameras and national identity cards may infringe on civil liberties, they do not necessarily raise questions of justice. We might call these "Orwellian preventives".

3) the idea of incapacitation, or keeping dangerous people in prison or jail based on notions of social defense, has many facets.

One must distinguish between incapacitation as a goal, that is, as the prime consideration, and incapacitation as a mere consequence of a sentence imposed on a retributive basis. To view incapacitation as a goal is to assume the role of controller and not to take the position of the one to be controlled. To view incapacitation as an incidental consequence of a sentence imposed on a different philosophical principle, fairness to the individual (retribution), and not as the goal in itself, is not to advocate the grounds of deterrence. Theories of retribution and their incidental deterrent effects will be discussed in a later chapter.

To prolong the period of imprisonment based on notions of incapacitation raises the issue of the very purpose of sentencing and of our priorities. We must consider whether we are interested primarily in justice to the individual offender or in the prevention of possible crime. An official committee in Sweden notes

The ethical problem is that incapacitation as a reason for penal intervention means that a person is punished not for what he has done but for what it is believed he may do in the future. A person exposed to a sanction that is more severe than that which the crime he committed usually entails, and justified by the fact that he is to be prevented from recidivating will thereby serve a sentence for a crime he did not commit and which in addition it is doubtful if he will ever commit. This conflicts with essential demands for legal security and can be compared to the sentencing of an innocent person.

(Quoted in Walker, 1991:59)

To the extent that nations or criminologists deviate from the above ethical standards they are placing other issues above the ideal of justice to the individual.

Perhaps even this idea of incapacitation should not properly be called deterrence, but individual prevention, which might also include such things as chemical castration for sexual offenders, or the sentencing of habitual offenders to life without parole upon the commission of any third felony. All of these raise questions about the legal securities of individuals in a constitutional democracy.

4) the prevention of crime due to the educating, moralizing aspect of law noted by Andenaes. (Andenaes, (1966) in Gerber and McAnany, 1972)

Johannes Andenaes notes that the distinction between individual or special prevention (the effects of punishment on the man being punished) and general prevention (the effects of punishment upon the members of society in general) is to some extent an artificial one insofar as if we fail to punish the individual offender, this may mal-educate the general population into the acceptability of such criminal behavior.

A prime consideration of Andenaes' argument for deterrence is the teaching effect that the punishment of offenders has on the general population, that it is wrong and unprofitable to break the law, and he calls this effect, general prevention. He argues that a society that fails to punish those who break the law may induce the law-abiding members also to break the law. Much of his argument is akin to Durkheim's argument that punishing offenders restates and reinforces the collective conscience of the good people. For Durkheim, the punishing of offenders keeps clear the line between acceptable and unacceptable behavior (Durkheim (1893), 1933). A strong moralistic sentiment would tend toward harsh punishments. It is only as moral prohibitions against particular behaviors diminish that punishments also diminish or disappear.

However, we must ask whether or not Durkheim is suggesting that the reverse is also true, that we may educate the masses by punishing offenses which they have not internalized as morally wrong. Evidence abounds that making something a crime and punishing those who break it does not seem to automatically induce mass obedience to that law. It is well known that the hanging of pickpockets did not seem to deter other pickpockets even at the public hanging of pickpockets. Likewise, laws outlawing the sale, distribution and consumption of alcohol in America in the 1920's were routinely violated. The current "war on drugs," which has overcrowded American prisons for the past twenty years, likewise does not seem to be effective in mass educating the public. The supply of illegal drugs, their distribution and use abounds.

Yet Andenaes argues that some behaviors may not be emotively internalized as *mala in se* (evil in themselves) and that in such areas where the law-breaker might calculate the cost and benefits of the crime (for example, tax evasion), strong punishments might be effective in producing law abidingness. Even if the individual offender is not deterred thereby, perhaps the general public will be educated, consciously or unconsciously, into law-abiding behavior.

While Andenaes openly rejects Benthamistic theories of deterrence, he does so only on the basis of Bentham's "shallow psychological" model of man as a rational calculator of consequences. But by advocating that the severity of the sentence should be based on its mass educational effectiveness, he puts himself clearly in the utilitarian perspective of Bentham. The criterion for deciding the severity of the sentence is its degree of effectiveness in reducing the crime rate, not whether the punishment is appropriate to the seriousness of the offense, not whether the individual being sentenced is being treated fairly and with consideration due to an equal human being. He is instead being treated as a mere means to Andenaes' ends, a mere example. Andenaes obscures this fact by paying lip service to notions of justice and fair treatment.

When the penalties are not reasonably attuned to the gravity of the violation, the public is less inclined to inform the police, the prosecuting authorities are less disposed to prosecute, and juries are less apt to convict.
(Andenaes in Gerber and McAnany, 1972:118)

For him, the political consequences of unjustly harsh exemplary
sentences are the only reasons sentences should be fair. Why others
should have a greater sense of fairness than does Andenaes is simply
not considered by him. Again, Andenaes seems to condemn "contemporary dictatorships that achieve great conformity through a "ruth-
lessly severe justice" (Andenaes in Gerber and McAnany, 1972). But
on what philosophic basis, other than on an unanalyzed emotive revulsion, they should be condemned is not addressed by him. What is
absolutely absent in Andenaes is any real consideration of why a sentence should be adjudged to be fair or otherwise. To shift the consideration of fairness to questions of the "moral" educating function of
sentence severity merely obscures the fact that the sentence must be
fair to the person being sentenced or it simply is not justice, except
perhaps in the narrow legal positivistic sense. In essence, Andenaes
displays the same crime controlling attitudes and assumptions as did
Bentham. This will become clearer in later discussions.

We have no problem with general education (prevention) arising
from fair sentencing as an incidental effect as long as it is not the
purpose of sentencing. If it is a purpose, it is treating the individual
as a means and not as an end. As long as the educational moral aspect of law occurs as an incidental bonus to a sentence imposed on
the decisive central criterion of justice to the individual, that is, a
fair punishment based on the seriousness of the crime committed,
then this should more properly be considered retribution theory and
is certainly quite different from criteria of efficient deterrence, general or particular.

5) deterrence properly so called; prevention of crime through fear of
punishment.

Deterrence can be defined as "the restraint which the fear of
criminal punishment imposes on those likely to commit crime . . ."
(Gerber and McAnany, 1972:93). Society comes to some agreement as to acts which should be prohibited, passes legislation to
that effect and establishes a penalty. It is the threat of the imposed

penalty and the fear thus engendered which is supposed to inhibit potential criminals and thereby protect society.

We will take the most widely held, albeit narrow, definition of deterrence as stated in number five above, the prevention of crime through fear of punishment, in order to clarify the intellectual roots and social consequences of this theory of deterrence.

The idea of deterrence as a justification of punishment has had many proponents through the years, the archetype of which is Thomas Hobbes with his Leviathan solutions briefly discussed earlier and whose theories deserve further elaboration in this chapter.

Since different theorists propose different justifications for criminal sentences, it may be enlightening, not only to discuss the relative merits and supporting arguments of the theories themselves, but to examine who says what, who proposes each kind of theory. Such an examination should include insights into the theorists' social position and intellectual assumptions and how these lead to his/her particular analysis.

As noted in chapter one, Thomas Hobbes had been educated in Oxford and was tutor to Lord Cavendish's family (Strauss, 1936). As such, his fortune and lifestyle were secure as long as the status quo of the society was not disturbed. Thus, the Puritan Revolts occurring at that time could easily be seen by him as a disturbing problem that could be done without. This is characteristic of all issues in the field of criminal justice. The concerns of the diverse theorists are often a product of their particular social status and the outcomes they desire. Clearly, the Puritan revolutionaries would not have seen themselves as the problem, but the status quo, which they wished to change. But given Hobbes' position in society, one can easily see that he wished to maintain undisturbed the domestic tranquility of his upper class lifestyle.

Hobbes was already a middle-aged man when he accidentally read Pythagoras' theorem in an opened book in a gentleman's library. Having read Pythagoras' theorem (the square of the hypotenuse is equal to the sum of the squares of the other two sides), he was amazed that this could be logically proven and so he read the book backwards to the beginning. This made him fall in love with the logic of geometry and the step by step proof. It seemed to him, more generally, that with the proper logical steps, the truth of all things could be deduced. This faith in the power of logic to arrive at the truth is known as scientific rationalism, which has continued to the present as part of our intellectual world view. It is reflected in the thinking of Hume, Locke, Bentham and even Arthur Conan Doyle's Sherlock Holmes.

Hobbes was both an acquaintance and admirer of Galileo (Bronowski and Mazlish:1960) and, as such, wished to explain the universe, and even, or should we say especially, man himself, purely in terms of matter in motion, a mechanical view of man. Since the commonly held view of a non-moving earth had been reliant upon the misinformation of the defective senses, it was easy to dismiss both that information and to generalize that dismissal to the general thinking of the common man.

Having dismissed the thinking of the common man as irrelevant, it now remained to reduce it to mere mechanism (Hobbes, (1651)1960). Since the primary (real) qualities of objects were those reducible to measurable quantities facilitating mathematical analysis and gave the real truth, the secondary qualities (those perceived through the senses: taste, color, odor, etc.), though irrelevant and misleading, still required explanation. For Hobbes, these secondary qualities do not exist in the body "out there," but exist solely in the *sensorium*, a specific part of the brain. They are thus a mere illusion caused there through the mechanical disturbance of its normal motions through impacts transmitted to it from the outside, always through other material motion in the human body. Since these secondary qualities do not exist in the object "out there," but exist merely in the *sensorium*, they are hence, simply unreal. Thus, he has essentially reduced the common man to a passive deluded puppet of the mechanical forces of nature, with little understanding of that which gives man his human dignity and equal respect. It is of small wonder that Hobbes engages in only a quest for control, not the human liberation of that deluded distainable puppet.

The Hobbesian Leviathan solutions to the problem of order in society have already been described in chapter one and merit only a brief reminder here. Hobbes, having "logically" deduced that man in the state of nature was selfish, mean and brutish, decides that man must appoint an absolute sovereign (a powerful government) to rule over him and to impose order on him through force and fear of punishment. But for the Leviathan, we would be at each other's throats. In essence, the only language we understand is fear of the Leviathan.

Why the Leviathan is to be exempted from the human condition of being by nature amoral is not explained by Hobbes. But, since he was a rewarded servant of the then ruling classes, it was easy for him to presume that they and the order they maintained were good.

One of the ways in which this fear of punishment was instilled in the masses was in the spectacle of public punishment, the infliction of pain that precipitated death. Michel Foucault ably describes this spectacle in his account of the sentence given Damiens on March 2, 1757, convicted for attempted regicide. As witnessed by Bouton, an officer of the watch on April 1, 1757, the sentence of Damiens involved

> the flesh torn from his breasts, arms, thighs and calves with red-hot pincers, his right hand, holding the knife with which he committed the said parricide, burnt with sulphur, and, on those places where the flesh will be torn away, poured molten lead, boiling oil, burning resin, wax and sulphur melted together and then his body drawn, and quartered by four horses and his limbs and body consumed by fire, reduced to ashes and his ashes thrown to the winds.
>
> (Quoted in Foucault, 1977:3)

This in fact was the only public part of the judicial process, for, as Foucault notes, in France and in most European countries, with the exception of England, "the entire criminal procedure, right up to the sentence, remained secret . . . not only to the public but also to the accused himself" (Foucault, 1977:35).

This entire process reflected the absolute power of Hobbes' Leviathan based on the theory of deterrence. There was no concern for the rights of the individual accused of criminal action; there was no concern for notions of justice or fairness. All that mattered was the power of the state. As Foucault notes,

> the entire procedure took place without him (the accused) . . . having any knowledge either of the charges or of the evidence. . . . Knowledge was the absolute privilege of the prosecution. . . . It was impossible for the accused to have access to the documents of the case, impossible to know the identity of his accusers, impossible to know the nature of the evidence before objecting to witnesses, impossible to make use, until the last moments of the trial, of the documents in proof, impossible to have a lawyer. . . .

> The magistrate . . . had the right to accept anonymous denunciations, to conceal from the accused the nature of the action, to question him with a view to catching him out, to use insinuations. . . . It was lawful for the judge to use false promises, lies, words with double meaning . . . (The judges) met with the accused only once in order to question him before passing sentence.
>
> (Foucault, 1977:35)

As Foucault succinctly notes in referring to the "solitary omnipotence" of the magistrate,

> The secret and written form of the procedure reflects the principle that in criminal matters, the establishment of truth was the absolute right and the exclusive power of the sovereign and his judges. . . . The King wished to show in this that the 'sovereign power' from which the right to punish derived could in no case belong to the 'multitude.' Before the justice of the sovereign, all voices must be stilled
>
> (Foucault, 1977:35–36)

It was the inherent unfairness of this criminal procedure that inspired Cesare Beccaria to write his book, *On Crimes and Punishments* (1764) and therein to propose a new system for the administration of criminal justice, based not on the omnipotent power of the sovereign, but on fairness and justice to the individual. We will discuss this in greater detail in the chapter on retribution.

This brutal and dehumanizing display of power presented as a public spectacle was clearly intended to intimidate any would be offenders from engaging in such crimes. However, the particular execution just detailed was not unique, but was given merely as an example of the contemporary common penal practices. Thus, Damiens knew the penalty, yet he committed the crime. Clearly, Damiens was not deterred from the commission of the crime. Nor, as noted earlier, did the hanging of pickpockets at Tyburn deter other pickpockets who were plying their trade during the hangings.

Such simplistic deterrence policies clearly assume that order in society must be imposed downwards from the ruling classes. The Hobbesian assumptions and problematics are clearly evident. The criminal justice system reflected securely established differentiated power and wealth in society, legitimated by the Divine Right of Kings.

It should be noted that all punishment systems develop in historical contexts, particular social structures and universes of discourse. By a universe of discourse, we mean the conceptions of reality, both articulated and assumed, together with their concomitant interests and concerns which are prevalent at a particular time and form the basis for conversations, discussions and plans among members of that universe. Over time, of course, the same universe of discourse may subdivide into somewhat different universes of discourse. For example, this same universe of discourse of those unified by faith in the indisputability of the truth of science subdivides. On one hand, it leads to scientific rationalism, which leads from Hobbes to Bentham and to the current technocrats of control. On the other hand, it also leads to a quite different notion of the right of the individual to think for himself unfettered by the powers of the church or the domination of monarchs. This latter, more humanistic path leads to the Enlightenment and a focus on civil rights and civil liberties.

But let us look more clearly at the historical context in which deterrence develops as a justification for punishment in the period between Hobbes (17th c.) and Bentham (19th c).

The power of the King and the power of the Church ruled supreme during the Middle Ages. This was a static society dominated by the ruling aristocracy in which one's place was ascribed at birth. No matter how creative or intelligent one might have been, if one were born a serf, one died a serf and one passed this status on to one's offspring. This was a culture of obedience, of domination and subjection, wherein the common man was required to obey both secular and religious powers and not to do so meant death or excommunication or both.

Gradually a new era dawned, the confidence in the truth of science, which in some views was available to all and in other views available only to the intelligentsia who despaired of the intellectual potential of the common man. Nevertheless, they agreed that the truth of science was not to be suppressed by either the power of the Church or the King.

Other influences fed into this new era. The voyages of discovery brought knowledge of new lands and different cultures, and the rediscovery of the writings of the Greeks contributed to a liberation of thought. In addition, the development of commerce and industry

facilitated by the technologies, the practical fruits of developments in
natural science, created a social base of power and wealth independent of the ownership of land on which feudalism was based. The au-
tocratic and despotic practices of the *Ancien Regime* were no longer
to be tolerated. Movements were initiated to protect one's liberty and
property. This other universe of discourse, driven by the ideals of the
Enlightenment, led to the overthrow of monarchy in the French and
American revolutions and planted the seeds of self-rule, democracy.
Ideally, this was no longer a society rooted in ascription, but one in
which man's achievements determined his role in society. Works like
Diderot's *Encyclopedia* (1751–1772) were now available to a broader
audience because of the invention of the printing press. The monopo-
lization of information and knowledge, which characterized the era
when books had to be copied by hand, was ending. Some indeed became interested in the philosophy of the Greeks and questions of individual rights and justice; others were far more interested in becom-
ing technocrats. These two universes of discourse, present in the 18th
century, continue to the present day.

Any transformations in the social structure, especially in the re-
distributions of power and wealth, require legitimations, re-definitions
of reality and changes in the laws. Since the rising industrial commercial classes could not appeal to notions such as the Divine Right of
Kings as justification for their position in society, new ideologies had
to be developed involving notions of the rights of the individual to autonomy of thought and action and to private property. Since it was this
last which was of paramount importance in legitimating their position
and resulting social relations, it seems to have been developed to a
greater extent than the former.

Thus private property became redefined. In the words of Blackstone, the right of private property entailed,

> the sole and despotic dominion which one man claims and exercises
> over the external things of the world, in total exclusion of the right of
> any other individual in the universe.
>
> (Blackstone, (1769) 1906: Book II: 207)

Locke described the right of private property as that which nature
and God has inscribed in the heart of man (Locke, (1690) 1924, chapter V). This new definition radically transformed previous, medieval

conceptions of the right of property, as, for example, that of St. Thomas Aquinas, who said that the right of private property did not have its roots in either divine commandment nor laws of nature. It was a human agreement created to promote other social benefits. Further, Aquinas noted that one was entitled to take what one needed and, if one took what one needed, it was not theft (Aquinas, vol. 2, (1481) 1947). A more modern statement of this medieval view of private property can be found in the writings of Pope John Paul II who has written that the goods of the earth were created by God for the use of mankind and nobody should be excluded from the necessities of life. God did not put the goods here for the benefit of the few. (Pope John Paul II, *Sollicitudo Rei Socialis*, 1987. (See also Pope John XXIII, *Mater et Magistra*, 1961)

But the new ideology of private property formulated by Blackstone and Locke legitimated private property as an absolute right with no consideration of the common good or fraternal obligations. In fact, this new definition of the right of private property meant that the gentry were disregarding common rights which they had formerly accepted as part of the "binding order of custom in the countryside" (Ignatieff, 1978:17).

Transformations in social structures often produce an array of casualties of that transformation. It is a curious habit of those whose livelihoods remain secure to ignore the plight of those displaced and, in essence, to perceive the victim as the problem. Thus, when the serfs were displaced from the land, their long established livelihood ended by new technologies of agriculture and commercial opportunities for the landowners, they were reduced to vagrancy, begging and theft for subsistence. The townspeople, the free tradesmen, often closed the gates of the towns against them. Poor laws were passed essentially making it a crime to be poor and be here. Yet these same free tradesmen were likewise later displaced from their home industries by being unable to compete with the new industrialized factories and mills and were in turn to join the ranks of the property-less and rioters.

In the enclosure of the commons, land previously available for common use was cordoned off as the private preserve of the King and his aristocracy for their pleasure, namely, the recreational sport of hunting red deer. It was not uncommon for leaseholds to be seized and turned into private parks or fishing ponds. Thus, the resources of the land,

reeds for thatching, rushes for lights and for floor covering, furze for
fuel and winter feed for cattle, peat for fuel, beech mast for feeding
hogs, stones for building. As well as nuts, berries mushrooms, truffles,
herbs, . . . crab apples, birds, rabbits . . .

(Hill, 1997:28)

that previously had been held in common, available to the ordinary vil-
lager, were now closed off and anyone who dared to enter this enclosed
space was subject to imprisonment or even death. In fact, in England, under the Black Act (1723), activities not previously defined as criminal
were now penalized, such as: stealing hedges, fruit from trees, timber,
damaging orchards, or taking fish from ponds (Thompson, 1975). The
number of crimes made capital offenses and hence punishable by death
increased from about 50 in 1688 to over 200 by 1820, and almost all of
these were for crimes against property (Hay, in Hay et al., 1975:18). Driven from their homes by force and violence, many became vagabonds.
But the Vagrancy Act, enacted in 1744, outlawed vagabondage by crimi-
nalizing the actions of beggars, gypsies, and peddlers. forcing them to
work as wage laborers in the newly forming factories and commercial
businesses (Ignatieff, 1978: 25). Thus, criminal sanctions were the means
used to reinforce the gentry's acclaimed right to property.

Other actions threatening to commerce, such as forgery and coun-
terfeiting, were likewise defined as capital offenses in response to demands by commercial and banking interests to protect the new systems
of paper credit and exchange. In fact, throughout the 18th century, two-
thirds of forgers were executed, a punishment akin to the crime of murder (Ignatieff, 1978:17).

Deterrence seems to have been the primary goal of these penalties.
In 1775 England, Matthew Normanton, a maker of counterfeit coin,
was hanged in chains for the murder of a tax man who had discovered
his offense. The justices noted that they had been urged to take the un-
usual step of hanging in chains by the respectable Gentlemen and Merchants who felt that 'such a notorious and public example' would deter others from making counterfeit coin (Cited in Ignatieff, 1978:17).
And again, two printers, Anderton and Dudley, while on the gallows of
Tyburn, condemned for high treason, were exhorted by the parson "to
beg of God they might be examples of true Repentance and to warn the
people by their sad untimely end" (Quoted in Ignatieff, 1978:23).

As Foucault has noted,

> In the ceremonies of the public execution, the main character was the people, whose real and immediate presence was required for the performance. An execution that was known to be taking place, but which did so in secret, would scarcely have had any meaning. The aim was to make an example, not only by making people aware that the slightest offense was likely to be punished, but by arousing feelings of terror by the spectacle of power letting its anger fall upon the guilty person . . .
> (Foucault, 1977:57–58)

Whippings and the pillory were also orchestrated for public effect, but this depended on the sentiments of the crowd who was the subject of this deterrent effect. Interestingly, despite the severity of the punishments at this time, many examples exist of the futility of these punishments in terms of deterrence. In fact, sometimes it backfired, as in the case of the aged radical printer, Daniel Isaac Eaton, who instead of instilling shame, was brought refreshments and garlanded with flowers at his pillorying. It was the magistrates and police who were reviled (Ignatieff, 1978).

Throughout this period, the magistrates, at the behest of the propertied interests, imposed more and more severe penalties, finally adding dissection to the penalty of hanging, hoping this would deter those would be criminals who wanted to have their bodies intact for all eternity. Instead of this having a deterrent effect, crime continued to escalate and the corpse became a commodity which could be bought and sold to the surgeons for surgical practice (Linebaugh, in Hay et al., 1975).

These policies of deterrence were not only proving to be ineffective, but were alienating and raising the ire of the common people, many of whom felt that the social structure and the legal system were unfair. At the public executions of some of those who led movements for change or who flouted laws deemed unfair to the common people, the multitude showed their support of the condemned and rioted against the authorities and their agents. In fact, after the execution of the silk weavers who had cut looms during the Spitalfields agitation of 1769, the Tyburn crowd rioted and destroyed the sheriff's house, not only because they felt that the offenders had been wrongfully put to death but also because their rights had been ignored. The sheriff had not given the men time to say their prayers and this was one of the rights of the dying defined by the poor of London (Ignatieff, 1978).

Another way in which the people showed their growing disaffection with the harshness of the criminal code was for juries to find those charged with grand larceny (a capital offense) guilty of only petty larceny instead (punishable with transportation), by valuing the goods stolen at less than a shilling, regardless of their true value. This was quite a common practice after 1750 (Ignatieff, 1978).

Thus, some 18th century observers began to doubt the effectiveness of public punishments (hangings, whippings, the pillory) as a deterrent policy. Clearly, new methods of control had to be created, one of which was transportation. By the late 1760's, seventy percent of all sentences at the Old Bailey were for transportation to the American colonies for terms of seven, fourteen years or life (Ignatieff, 1978:20). Indeed, transportation had many advantages over the former public punishments. It provided cheap labor for the propertied classes in the colonies; it peopled the colonies (America and Australia) with English citizens, thus contributing to the expansion of the Empire; it got rid of troublemakers at home; and when the Crown commuted the sentence of hanging to transportation, it made the Crown appear merciful.

Nevertheless, it was the development of the prison, which was increasingly viewed as a way out of the public humiliation accorded the authorities when the crowds supported the criminal rather than the law. By isolating the criminal, removing him from public view, the gallows could no longer be the rallying point of the criminal classes, the poor, the property-less and the vagrants who were increasingly showing their solidarity with the condemned. The gallows could no longer serve as a symbol for the injustice of this new social order based on the rights of property for a few, perhaps as few as three percent of the population of England at the time. (Hay, in Hay et al., 1975:61)

It is interesting to note how the industrial commercial class's assertion of their own property rights tended to displace older concepts of common law which protected the people's rights to the resources of the commons. This assertion of private property rights also tended to displace other considerations of the Enlightenment, such as notions of human rights and the dignity of man. How simplistically they assumed that order could be imposed from above through force and fear—the old Hobbesian Leviathan with new rulers!

THE PRISON AS DETERRENT

There are diverse, mixed and often conflicting goals given for penal policies. As such, prison as an institution can be based on different ideologies.
It can be viewed as punishment (retribution), deterrence, or might form
the setting for policies based on rehabilitation. It can be based on notions
of nurture, (retribution and the Pennsylvania Model) or nature, (Pentonville and the Auburn Model). Here we are primarily concerned with
the influences of the nature perspective on incarceration. Thus, prison can
be viewed as part of the control apparatus used by the men of property to
control the property-less and force their entry into the new social order of
the times, based on industrialization and the rights of men of property. As
such, prison can also be viewed as a precaution against further political
and social unrest, by isolating the offenders from public view.

Prison was rarely used as a form of punishment prior to the latter
part of the 18th century. Instead, prisons were used to confine debtors
and their families until debts were paid, to serve as workhouses for the
poor (bridewells) and to detain those awaiting trial and sentencing.

The largest debtors' prisons were in London. Here his family could remain with the debtor until the debt was paid or "they were discharged as
insolvent by an act of Parliament." (Ignatieff, 1978:29) They were not
confined to a cell and hence were free to receive visitors from the outside.
They could not be chained nor forced to work. Thus, the plight of Mac-
Cawber in Charles Dicken's novel, *David Copperfield*, (1852) provides a
glimpse into a debtors' prison. Moreover, in some prisons, you could purchase separate quarters from the keeper; otherwise men and women were
housed together. Some keepers augmented their pay by selling the privi-
lege of living outside the prison walls or the right to leave the prison during the daylight hours. Some maintained a coffee shop and tap room for
prisoners and visitors. Discipline was not a problem, immorality was. Li-
centiousness and drunkenness abounded.

Another form of custody was the bridewell, or house of correction,
a workhouse for the poor instituted to get vagrants off the streets. Contract labor was initiated whereby outside entrepreneurs contracted with
the bridewell management to have goods produced by the cheap labor
of the inmates thus providing commercial opportunities for the entrepreneurs and managers of the bridewell while saving the propertied
classes the expense of custodializing the poor.

Brickmakers used bridewell prisoners to beat bricks into dust; candle-
makers set them to making candlewick; wood merchants employed
them chipping logwood; masters in the iron trade set them to making
butchers' skewers; and mattress makers contracted for their labor as
feather pickers . . .

(Quoted in Ignatieff, 1978:32)

In theory, prisoners were to earn their keep by this contract labor
but, in fact, because of the rapid turnover of prisoners and their lack of
skill and diligence, it was difficult to make a profit, and hence many
entrepreneurs simply defaulted on their contracts. The result was enforced idleness, drunkenness, and debauchery. Disobedience was punished by lashes or being chained standing for up to twenty-four hours
at a time. If one were too poor to provide one's own food, or had no
relations to turn to, one could starve to death.

Conditions in the jails were no better. Most were in the dungeons
of medieval castles and held debtors and their families, felons and
misdemeants awaiting trial, and those awaiting transportation, min-
gling freely with one another. In fact, some of those acquitted of
their alleged crime languished in jail because they did not have the
money to pay the keeper a "discharge fee" to break their fetters (Ignatieff, 1978:31). Disease was rampant and was often blamed on the
immorality and lack of discipline of the poor. As noted in a pamphlet
on jail fever in 1773, "filth and disease were as natural to the poor .
. . as cleanliness and health were to the virtuous and industrious"
(Ignatieff, 1978:60).

The degrading and licentious conditions of the debtors' prisons,
bridewells and jails perturbed a goodly number of deeply religious
non-conformists (Quakers and Unitarians). They were also members
of the new commercial industrialist class who had great faith in scientific rationality and technology, men like James Watt and Matthew
Boulton (proprietors of the Soho Engineering Works in Birmingham,
England), Abraham Darby (iron and steel magnate), and Josiah
Wedgewood (pottery magnate). In fact, it was their faith in rationality,
which justified human autonomy in the quest for truth in science,
which also led to their belief in human autonomy in deciding one's dis-
senting religious faith. Both these influences (religious belief and scientific rationality) converge in the creation of a new penal system to

replace the floggings, executions, and transportations that were proving not only unproductive, but could also incite the property-less to increasing social unrest.

The type of prison system that evolved owed much to the scientific, industrial and religious background of the reformers. While they supported many philanthropic causes, such as the abolition of slavery, construction of hospitals and dispensaries and schools for the poor, they were best known for the development of scientific management in the factories (Ignatieff, 1978:62). They were convinced of the need to instill good moral virtues in the poor and they were convinced of the connection between discipline, morality, cleanliness and law-abiding behavior. In fact, these reformers often referred to humans as "machines to be tinkered with and improved" (Ignatieff, 1978:68). Josiah Wedgewood boasted that "he would make machines of men as cannot err" (Quoted in Ignatieff, 1978; 68).

The Englishman, John Howard, fervent Quaker and influential prison reformer, was further influenced by his travels abroad and by his study of prisons on the continent, which he found to be clean and quiet. The notion of monastic discipline, solitary confinement and silent penance was gleaned from his travels to a Vatican prison for young juveniles, built in 1703. From Amsterdam, he borrowed ideas of uniforms (originally for purposes of hygiene), confinement in cells, constant inspection, and fixed times for meals, work and prayer (Ignatieff, 1978). All of these ideas come together in the creation of the Pentonville penitentiary opened in London in 1842.

The Pentonville model, with its factory system, combined ideas of religious conversion with faith in the technology and molding of men through regimentation to the clock and schedules of work.

Pentonville was built on a six acre site and was surrounded by walls, twenty-five feet in height. Cells were constructed in tiers of three, and were approximately 13ft by 7ft by 9ft. Each cell contained a table, chair, cobbler's bench, hammock, broom, bucket and corner shelf. On the shelf stood a pewter mug and dish, bar of soap, towel and a Bible. Except for exercise and chapel, a convict spent his entire day and night in solitary confinement in that cell (Ignatieff, 1978). Even in chapel, the convicts, isolated in solitary boxes, were constantly upbraided about the horrible conditions of their souls and threatened with eternal damnation if they did not reform.

The day began with the clanging of a bell at 5:45 AM. The convict had 15 minutes to be ready for inspection, dressed in his uniform, room tidied and at work at his cobbler's bench or loom. Inmates worked eight and one-half hours a day, in solitary confinement. The monotony of work was broken only with mandatory attendance at chapel and meals, which were passed through a trap door in the cell (Ignatieff, 1978). The prison was run like a machine and the inmate virtually cut off from any contact with either the world outside the prison or any human contact within.

In America, in 1776, Jonah Hanway, a Pennsylvania Quaker and associate of John Howard, drew the plan for one of the first prisons in the New World, not so much for punishment as for reformation. As such, it incorporated many of the same ideas found later in Pentonville. Solitary confinement and discipline were the foundation stones of both systems. It was believed that meditation and reflection on one's past life would lead to repentance and a resolve not to offend nor sin again, while the discipline of work would be a deterrent to crime. Thomas Eddy, a New York Quaker, applied these same ideas to the construction of Newgate Prison in New York State in 1796 (Lewis, 1965).

Nevertheless, the Pennsylvania model prison of Jonah Hanway had fewer inmates (200 as compared to the 450 of Pentonville) and larger cells (24ft, by 29ft, by 14ft). Work was performed at a small bench in the cell, but was not organized on the factory system as observed later at Pentonville. Since it was of an artisan nature, labor could not be economical; it was instead considered to be therapeutic (Melossi and Pavarini, 1981). Spiritual needs took precedence. Individual walled gardens were provided for the physical exercise of the inmates and were reached by passageways similar to the ones which led to the chapel situated in the center of the prison. Inmates exercised alone and observed religious services from this passageway undetected by fellow inmates.

Anonymity pervaded the Pennsylvania model to the greatest degree possible. Prisoners were unknown to each other, outsiders and guards except by number. An 1837 report of the New Jersey Board of Inspectors concluded that the Pennsylvania model was "undoubtedly the most humane and civilized system known" (Melossi and Pavarini, 1981:127). [See also, Lewis, (1965) and Rothman, (1971, 1980)].

The Pennsylvania Model with its emphasis on solitude in which to reflect on one's past evil deeds and thereby hopefully to achieve religious conversion, contains elements of the nurture approach to man. Man was viewed, at least in part, as a free thinking, reasonable individual capable of changing one's life from one of crime to one of law-abidingness.

The modifications made later at Pentonville perhaps mirrored the different population of inmates (urban as opposed to rural), the growth of the factory system and the concern with the number of cases of insanity, which seemed to accompany the prolonged solitary confinement of the Pennsylvania model.

In America, the Pennsylvania model soon became discredited perhaps because of the incidences of insanity, but also because of the lack of productivity of the prisoners and the cost of the relatively spacious cells. It was replaced with the Auburn model, which took its name from the city in which it was developed, Auburn, New York. The most distinctive feature of the Auburn System was its virtual rejection of any of the reform ideals of the Quakers. Solitude and meditation were replaced with a pragmatic concern for financial solvency, security and custody.

The Auburn model was to reflect in part the character and beliefs of the residents of Auburn, emigrants from New England, who believed strongly in law, temperance, hard labor, and the establishment of churches and schools (Lewis, 1965). These were Calvinists, who believed that all men were tainted with original sin but from the beginning of time some were predestined to be saved and others were predestined to eternal damnation. No one could change his/her fate. Those predestined to damnation were viewed as particularly dangerous to civilized society, for they had nothing to lose by engaging in crime and sinfulness. This was very different from the beliefs of the Quakers who held that man has free will and thus is capable of redemption should he choose the path to God.

For the Calvinists, those saved would manifest this state of salvation by affluence in this world and salvation in the next. Thus, the poor did not arouse sympathy from the affluent, but were viewed as "dangerous," preying on their fellow man and needing the criminal law to "terrify them into a respect for other people's property" (Rennie, 1978:54). Here, instead of notions of the nurture approach to man, we see instead more of a nature approach focusing on deterrence and control of the dangerous classes.

Rennie has noted,

The law did not apply such draconian measures to the rich. At first blush, this seems surprising, since the mighty, no less than the humble, were supposedly corrupted by Adam's original sin. However, the view of the criminal law seems to have been that because of the easier circumstances of their lives, the vicious rich were less subject to temptation and hence less dangerous than the vicious poor. Their offenses did not, and to this day do not, exact the same harsh penalties from the law—a net that has always and everywhere been woven to catch minnows and let the sharks swim free. (This becomes more understandable when one reflects that it is the great, and not the small, fish who design the net.)

(Rennie,1978: 54)

In Auburn, cells were small, approximately 7ft by 3ft by 7ft, arranged back to back and in tiers five cells high. The tiers of cells were arranged as an island in the center of the structure with a vacant area 11 feet wide surrounding all four sides of the "island." Enclosing the island and the area around it was an outer shell pierced by small windows affording some degree of light. It was thus, a prison within a prison, for an outside wall surrounded the entire institution (Lewis, 1965).

As would later be the case at Pentonville, the congregate labor of inmates was an important part of the penal system. At Auburn, it was the duty of prison administrators to find businessmen willing to put their raw materials into the hands of convicts to be later marketed at the risk of business. Thus, by 1826, approximately a dozen contracts involving the manufacture of: shoes, rifles, tools, clothes and the metal rings for barrels (coopering) had been signed by the prison administrators at Auburn (Lewis, 1965: 180). The factory system had come to the prison and the inmate had become an economic slave.

Jenkins notes that the purpose of prison labor was to train workers for the factory system, developing in force outside the prison system (Jenkins, 1984:170). Nevertheless, while the Auburn model in America had prison industries and an incipient factory system operating within prison walls, there is no evidence that the primary goal was the preparation of inmates for future employment outside the prison. In America, the overriding goal of prison industry was that the prison be economically self sufficient, paying for itself with the labor of its inmates. If prison industry also achieved the goal of work discipline, that would have been considered a beneficial by-product (Lavin-McEleney, 1985:12–15). There was little interest in the inmate's soul, only his labor as a source of profit to the system.

To maintain discipline and order, a strict silence code prevailed at all times, even at meals. Elaborate techniques for constant surveillance, coercion and intimidation were viewed as a necessary ingredient of security. Flogging was also a part of prison discipline. Some of these control techniques were a result of the military experiences of the Auburn prison staff who had served in the War of 1812 (Lewis,1965). Marching manoeuvres, such as the lock step, whereby inmates marched single file each placing his right hand on the shoulder of the man in front of him, were used to transfer inmates from one part of the institution to another. The classification of guards as Sergeants, Lieutenants, and Captains in the upper ranks again serves to confirm the paramilitary organization of the prison—a legacy which holds true today in the 21st century.

Michel Foucault makes an interesting analogy between this mechanization of human behavior and the mechanization discovered in nature by the men of science. The following statements by Foucault thus clarify the 18th century legacy of science and the resultant deterministic (nature) view of man (a quest for cause-effect sequences) as it is reflected in penal policy.

Foucault states,

> side by side with the major technology of the telescope, the lens and the light beam, which were an integral part of the new physics and cosmology, there were minor techniques of multiple and intersecting observations . . . preparing a new knowledge of man. These (human) 'observatories' had an almost ideal model: the military camp. In the perfect camp, all power would be exercised solely through exact observation; each gaze would form a part of the overall functioning of power.
>
> (Foucault, 1977:171)

Approximately one hundred and fifty years after Hobbes, Bentham's conception of the Panopticon was thus to resurrect the ideal of the Leviathan and thus form the theoretical base for a policy of control, of power over the kept—deterrence and social defense in action. The

Inspectors' Report of Auburn Prison in 1822 was to reaffirm the pre-eminence of control over reformation.

> The great end and design of criminal law is the prevention of crimes, through fear of punishment; the reformation of offenders being a minor consideration
>
> (Quoted in Lewis, 1965:63).

JEREMY BENTHAM—THE FATHER OF UTILITARIANISM

Because Jeremy Bentham provides the theoretical base for so much of deterrence and social defense theory, a further analysis of his ideas is warranted.

The faith in the incontrovertible truth achieved by scientists such as Galileo, and Newton had somewhat different implications for different thinkers. For some, it legitimated the freedom of the human mind from the external and coercive constraints politically imposed by popes or monarchs on the human quest for truth. For many of the religiously inclined it implied that no coercive constraints or penalties should be imposed on individuals even in the choice of religious beliefs. This was particularly appealing to the religious dissenters whose loyalty to the monarchy was doubted due to their break from the established Church of England, headed by the sovereign. Freedom of religion from coercive restraints would mean an end to the religious persecutions and discriminations they had suffered. This, and similar considerations, influenced their quest for specifying human rights, which found its political expression in the French Declaration of the Rights of Man and the Citizen and the American Constitution's statement on the freedom of religion.

For others, the faith in the incontrovertibility of the truth of science had the much narrower implications of the nature approach as described in chapter one. It meant both the faith in a mechanical view of the universe, purged of any considerations of human creativity or will, and the quest to find the natural forces or mechanisms at work in producing even human thought and human behavior. It meant that a deterministic quantifiable science of absolutely everything was both possible and desirable. Especially it meant that the enlightened possessors of such a science of man could, and should, use their expertise to control and manipulate others, presumably benevolently. Such were the views and goals of Jeremy Bentham, one of the acknowledged fathers of the field of modern criminal justice, often quoted but too little critiqued.

Bentham, born in 1748, was a child prodigy, studying Latin at the age of four and thereafter French and the violin. He entered Oxford University at the age of twelve, graduating at fifteen and entering law school. But, as often happens to the precociously gifted, his sociable interactions with others and his practical experience of life were correspondingly diminished. As an adult, the possession of an independent income freed him from not only the necessity of earning a living but also from the day to day social contacts which that would entail. He never married, met people "only for some specific purpose," and labeled himself "the hermit of Queens' Square Place" (Bronowski and Maslish, 1960:473).

He had complete faith that there could be a scientific understanding of everything, including even of the moral and practical life of man, which was to be seen as the effect of mere natural mechanisms. Bentham clearly accepted the nature view of man, which is evident in his disagreements with Blackstone.

Shortly after the fifteen year old Bentham entered law school, he listened to the lectures of Blackstone, who claimed that the purpose of law was to delineate the correspondence of rights and duties of individuals in society. Essentially these rights and duties for Blackstone were enshrined in the established common law and supported by concepts of natural rights such as the natural absolute right to private property, a view which rigidified and legitimated the static status quo.

Bentham immediately found himself in profound disagreement with Blackstone. But rather than assailing Blackstone's narrow and legalistic views of the concept of natural rights and pursuing their elaboration and extension through further consideration, Bentham simply rejected the concept of natural rights completely and attacked the very concept of rights in his subsequent writings.

For Bentham, rights simply had no scientific basis. Even the American Declaration of Independence and the French Declaration of the Rights of Man and of the Citizen he considered "meaningless hodge podges" insofar as they were based on the concept of rights of the individual. (Bronowski and Maslish, 1960:433)

Having rejected the specification of rights and duties of individuals as the purpose of law, what then was to be its purpose? For his answer, Bentham drew on the writings of Hume and Locke and "Montesquieu, Barrington, Beccaria, and Helvetius, but most of all Helvetius, set me on the principle of utility" (Bronowski and Maslish, 1960:434). Bentham distilled this notion of utility into his assertion that ". . . the greatest happiness of the greatest number is the foundation of all morals and legislation" (Bronowski and Maslish, 1960:434).

At first sight, this greatest happiness principle would seem to have a certain amount of appeal. Should not the aim of government and legislation seek to make as many as happy as possible?

But a more careful analysis illustrates the serious fallacy of Bentham's claim. As William James notes, making the happiness of the many dependent on the misery of one is ethically unacceptable. (James, 1956:188) Perhaps a hypothetical example, which is not original but whose authorship we are unable to locate, will show just how unacceptable is Bentham's "greatest happiness for the greatest number" criterion.

Suppose a spaceship lands, extraterrestrials emerge and put to us the following proposal. "We have the technology: to cure all diseases, to extend the human lifespan to 200 years, to eliminate famine and war, to create abundant supplies of all consumer goods effortlessly, to control the weather and all natural disasters. We will give you all this in exchange for one thing. We ourselves have lived so securely and pain-free that we are somewhat bored and have become fascinated with observing someone in pain. All we want in exchange for our technology is one seven year old child whom we will keep in exquisite agony every second for the next 200 years."

Think about it- the elimination of all childhood cancers, all pain and suffering in the world! Should we take the deal for the greatest happiness of the greatest number?

But let us consider the proposal further. First, should I sacrifice this child if I alone were going to benefit from it? Clearly that would be barbarously unethical, a crime akin to (worse than) murder. Second, could I give permission to you to accept that deal on my behalf and for my benefit? Clearly the answer must be "no" since I can not ethically accept it on my own behalf, I can not ethically give you permission to do it for me. Third, can you ethically accept it for me without my knowledge and consent? Again the answer is "no". This would be doubly unethical insofar as you have made a decision for me that I would consider unethical and you have unethically deprived me of my right to make a decision. In such a case, you do not have, and I cannot give you, the authority to speak for me. By extension, this means that no one may decide for anyone else, not even for the greatest happiness of the greatest number, in this matter. Each of us must speak for himself or herself.

But if you accept the nature view of man, which Bentham did, on what basis would you reject this deal? If man is reduced to a mere product of nature, caused to act by forces of nature, devoid of intelligence and will, then is there any basis on which to reject this deal? We can only reject the deal if we acknowledge man as interpreter of reality, creator of values and developer of his own character, as outlined in chapter one. Indeed, our happiness depends on the achievement of the values we have created, whether holiness, truthfulness, loyalty, wealth, or justice. In accepting the deal, each of us would know that we had treated that child unfairly. On the other hand, Bentham's view of man is devoid of any values, "call them soldiers, call them monks, call them machines, so they were but happy ones, I should not care" (Quoted in Spragens, 1981:111). Bentham, believing in a mechanistic view of man, desirous of the greatest good for the greatest number, logically would not be able to reject the deal offered by the visitors from space, especially if the beneficiaries could be left ignorant of its conditions.

While this example shows the fallacy of the concept of the "greatest good for the greatest number" as a statement of the purpose of government and legislation, it also highlights the importance of having a democracy based on informed choice and consent.

Incidentally, it might be noted that notions of social defense involving the protection of society from potentially dangerous people without regard to the rights of those dangerous people for fair treatment suffers from the same defects as Bentham's "greatest happiness for the greatest number" principle. But we will return to the concept of social defense later in this chapter.

Moreover, how scientific was Bentham? When asked to prove his confidently asserted principle about the purpose of government and legislation being for the greatest good for the greatest number, he found himself unable to give proof. He merely asserts that its truth was self evident without further analysis. Yet here Bentham is dealing with one of the deepest and most fundamental of human questions—the purpose of life itself, the question which has engaged the greatest philosophers and theologians throughout the ages. Yet Bentham, preoccupied with his reductionist view of man as a mere puppet to be controlled, misses the universal human quest for the very meaning of life.

Bentham, having decided that the very content of the laws should be to produce the greatest happiness for the greatest number, then has to engage in finding the mechanisms to make us obey these laws. Here again, we find Bentham's reductionist view of man. He claims that man is rational and operates to maximize pleasure and minimize pain. Some writers, quoting Bentham's reference to human rationality, assume that since individuals make decisions, Bentham recognized the existence of human free will. But such is clearly not the case. Bentham clearly states, "Nature has placed mankind under the governance of two sovereign masters, pain and pleasure " (Bentham, (1789) 1948;1) Pleasure and pain are the ultimate deciders. Man, then, is reduced to a mere calculator of pleasure and pain.

> . . . When matters of such importance as pain and pleasure are at stake, and these in the highest degree(the only matters, in short, that can be of importance) who is there that does not calculate? Men calculate, some with less exactness, indeed, some with more: but all men calculate. . . .
> (Bentham, (1789) 1948:187–188)

Bentham assumes that the decision is pre-set in the amount of pleasure or pain consequent upon a particular course of behavior and that we simply declare the answer in exactly the same way that an electronic calculator simply states the answer to a mathematical sum. The electronic calculator has no free will. It calculates but does not decide. It merely declares.

Based on this view of man, Bentham now proceeds to set up his system of criminal laws whereby the breaking of any law will incur more pain than the pleasure that is to be gained from the offense. Here we have a clear statement of deterrence, the idea that people are to be coerced into law abidingness by the threat of pain that Bentham wants to make effective through notions of its severity, certainty and proximity to the crime. Again, we have slipped into an updated Hobbesian notion that the purpose of the criminal law is coercion rather than justice.

The amount of pain to be attached to the breaking of a particular law, for example, burglary, is to be derived scientifically, calculated in terms of its effectiveness. Thus, Bentham proposes the gathering of crime statistics in order to adjust the pain to its maximum efficiency. He recognized that beyond a certain amount, it would take more and more pain to produce smaller amounts of increase in law abidingness. Thus, when Bentham seems to be against the use of the infliction of excessive pain, he is not being a kind humanitarian, but merely an economist. It is interesting to note that the gatherers of the first statistics on crimes, Quetelet and Guerry, acknowledge that their work was at Bentham's suggestion. Today, much time and effort is given to the gathering of crime statistics, seemingly for unanalyzed Benthamistic purposes.

We have deliberately avoided the use of the word "punishment" as the word "punishment" has different philosophical connotations. It is at least doubtful whether a lawbreaker could be considered morally culpable given Bentham's reductionistic (amoral) view of man. Bentham's infliction of pain on his puppet version of man is more akin to a Newtonian force operating on a moving object.

Bentham particularly liked the idea of imprisonment as pain insofar as it was very adjustable in duration for purposes of determining its maximum efficiency in forcing law abidingness. He called his planned penitentiary, the "Panopticon," which was designed so that the convicted would be housed in a myriad of individual cells constructed around a central observation tower. From the interior of this tower, the keepers clandestinely could watch every movement of the kept. This was the all-seeing eye that made chains and physical restraints unnecessary. Convicts were to be employed as long as sixteen hours a day in their cells and all profits would accrue to the manager of the penitentiary—Bentham himself (Bentham, (1791) 1962).

Bentham's description of his convict laborers gives no doubt of his image of man as a puppet to be controlled.

> What other master is there that can reduce his workmen, if idle, to a situation next to starving, without suffering them to go elsewhere? What other master is there whose men can never get drunk unless he chooses they do so?
>
> (Bentham, *Panopticon*, (1791) 1962:56)

(See also Ignatieff, 1978:109–113 and Foucault, 1977: chapter 3 Panopticism)

It is interesting to note that Bentham saw the Panopticon also as an ideal laboratory in which different types of criminals could be segregated and studied by social scientists to find effective rehabilitative measures. Of course, given his puppet version of man, what matters to Bentham is to find ways to control that puppet. There is thus a compatibility between the deterministic nature approach version of rehabilitation and notions of scientific deterrence. Although often taken as opposing ideas, both rehabilitation and scientific deterrence are interested in questions of control, rather than questions of justice or liberty.

INDIVIDUAL DETERRENCE—SOCIAL DEFENSE

Modern notions of scientific deterrence, notions of scientific rehabilitation and notions of incapacitation are usually legitimated by reference to notions of social defense. As Marc Ancel has noted, the oldest conception of social defense was limited "to the protection of society by the repression of crime" and a more modern conception would be "the prevention of crime and the treatment of offenders" (Ancel, in Gerber and McAnany, 1972:133). Nevertheless, the main thrust of social defense is to protect "the public" by preventing the "dangerous" offender from further re-offending. Basically, this entails incapacitation with or without treatment (Ancel, in Gerber and McAnany, 1972:133).

How is the dangerous offender to be identified? The Model Sentencing Act proposed by the American criminal justice think tank, the National Council on Crime and Delinquency, in 1963 defined the dangerous offender as some one "suffering from a mental or emotional disorder indicating a propensity toward continuing criminal activity of a dangerous nature" (Quoted in Gerber and McAnany, 1972:151). The offender's past crime is used to predict his/her future criminal behavior. The basic assumption is that the dangerous offender cannot control his/her actions (nature approach) and must therefore be restrained in order to prevent him/her from further harm to others. This was a popular policy initiative in the 1960's and 1970's in the United States.

In the name of social defense, we incapacitate, or isolate the offender to prevent future re-offending. The policies based on social defense have taken many forms: preventive detention, whereby an individual judged to be dangerous could be denied bail and thus confined to a jail while awaiting trial; longer than usual sentences if the offender was judged to be a dangerous offender; and various other models of sentencing such as the "dual track system of punishment," which combined punishment with preventive detention, also known as "measures". All of these policies relied heavily on psychiatric and psychological evaluations in order to predict the offender's future dangerousness.

Helen Silving has described this dual track system of punishment that was in place in Germany and other parts of Europe in the 1960's (Silving in Gerber and McAnany, 1972). Typically, upon the expiration of his/her criminal sentence, the offender would be analyzed by a psychiatrist or psychologist to determine if, upon release, the offender was likely to be a danger to others. If determined to be a danger, the offender would continue to be confined indefinitely under terms called "measures" until he/she was found to be no longer a danger to the community. It is important to note that "measures" were not deemed to be punishment, (the criminal sentence handed down by the courts had already been served) but were designed to be "reformative, curative or protective" and as soon as the goal was achieved, the measure was terminated and the person could return to society. (Silving as quoted in Gerber and McAnany, 1972:144)

Again according to Silving,

> . . . the positivist school of criminal law . . . predicates state intervention into the individual sphere upon the 'social necessity' of community protection against danger emanating from the delinquent individual. Such protection is afforded by reformation of the reformable and confinement of the unreformable.
>
> (Silving in Gerber and McAnany, 1972:144)

It is important to reiterate that the individual is being confined beyond the length of the court sentence, not on the basis of a crime committed, but because of what he/she might do in the future. The awesome power of deciding between liberty or indefinite confinement was thus placed in the hands of psychiatrists and psychologists who were not a part of the legal system. For the most part, these evaluators operated from the nature perspective. Gone were notions of free will or responsibility or proportionality between the crime and the punishment or justice for the offender.

By the 1980's, in the United States and elsewhere, the validity of these psychiatric evaluations was being questioned, thus requiring a different mechanism for determining dangerousness. By the 1990's a much simpler means was utilized in order to identify the dangerous offender, one that required the judge to merely add up the number of prior felonies. If the individual before the judge had two prior felonies and was now convicted of a third felony, the sentence was automatic, life imprisonment without the possibility of parole. Thus, these so-called habitual offender laws were designed to keep the offender permanently isolated from society. He/she was presumed to be a criminal by habit, dangerous by nature. The period of incarceration was specified by a simple mathematical calculation.

Nevertheless, in the area of sexually violent predators, psychiatric evaluations were still being used at the beginning of the 21st century to justify extended commitment of an offender beyond the original term of imprisonment imposed by the court. We will return to this issue in the following chapter on rehabilitation.

One has only to consider the Texas case of William James Rummel (1978) to see that habitual offender laws are devoid of any consideration of justice or proportionality between the crime and the sentence. In total, Rummel's three non-violent felony convictions resulted in a theft of about $230, for which he is serving a sentence of life without parole, sanctioned by the Supreme Court of the United States. (Cited in Jenkins, 1984:172) In contrast, first time felon, Ivan Boesky received a ten year sentence for the theft of millions of dollars from innocent stock holders. Several federal court judges have descried the inequality inherent in these laws passed in the name of social defense (Statement by Robert W. Pratt, US District Court Judge for the Southern District of Iowa cited in Chambliss, 1999:26).

One of the ways of evaluating any of the aforementioned social theorists is by analyzing the theorist's social background and world experience, his/her values, and his/her level of respect for other human beings. Is he/she interested in justice for the individual and protection of individual freedom and autonomy or is he/she interested merely in control—control of the bad people by incapacitation and control of the good by way of general prevention.

No doubt Bentham did not see himself as a powerless individual concerned with protecting his rights against the possible abuse of power by the state but, rather as akin to, *mutatis mutandis*, the self righteous aristocracy who presumed their right and obligation to find and root out the evils they perceived in society. Note that the evils to be rooted out were typically found in the actions of the lower classes. All social defense principles partake of these same inclinations.

CONCLUDING THOUGHTS ON DETERRENCE

In conclusion, there are several questions to be raised about deterrence as we have defined it, the restraint from crime caused by fear of criminal punishment. These are: 1) does it work, 2) is it based on an adequate conception of man, 3) is it fair or just, 4) where does order in society come from?

The first question is, does it work? Does the severity of sentencing actually reduce crime rates? It is generally accepted that certainty of detection and punishment is of greater consequence in deterring people than is the severity of the sentence. For example, professional criminals, juvenile delinquents, and habitual offenders may be undeterred by the severity of a sentence and, as Andenaes correctly notes, "threats of future punishment, especially as apprehension is uncertain, do not have the same motivating power as the desires of the moment" (Andenaes (1966) in Gerber and McAnany, 1972:117). There is also evidence that, when the public perceives the punishment to be too severe, there is a tendency not to convict, as occurred in New York State with the Baumes Laws (Andenaes (1966) in Gerber and McAnany, 1972:118).

In England, for generations, pickpockets were hanged publicly. There was no corresponding decrease in pickpocketing. Indeed, public hanging of pickpockets, was seen as a challenge to the courage and skill of other pickpockets, who saw the distraction of the crowds as the perfect opportunity to ply their trade. There have been states that have alternated between periods when the death penalty was imposed for homicide and periods when such penalty was abolished. Studies have shown no difference in the homicide rate between these periods. (Sellin, 1980)

The passage of laws prohibiting alcoholic beverages (Prohibition) and massive efforts to enforce these laws appear to have been largely ineffective and may actually have led to a general increase in other kinds of crime. In the United States, the war on drugs and mandatory severe sentencing have been the norm for years, apparently to no greater effect than to increase the prison population and to disproportionately disenfranchise minorities.

In other cases, the entire apparatus of state police and military have been directed against insurgent rebels variously described as terrorists or liberation fighters, without any great success.

The United States has both the highest execution rates and the highest homicide rates of modern industrialized nations (Hudson, 1998:23). According to the U. S. Department of Justice, Bureau of Justice Statistics, between 1976 and 2003, the United States executed 885 people. In 1999, 98 criminals were put to death, the highest number since 1951. In the year 2002, the number of prisoners under sentence of death was 3,557 (Bureau of Justice Statistics (BJS), 2003). Most other nations of the world (108) have abandoned the death penalty, except perhaps for treason. America, India and Japan are the only industrial democracies to continue death penalties, but India and Japan's rate of use of the death penalty is much lower than that of the United States ("Executions", 2000). Interestingly, according to Amnesty International, in 1999, 85% of the world's executions occurred in the United States, China, Congo, Iran and Saudi Arabia ("Executions", 2000).

And yet recent issues surrounding executions in America highlight problems with deterrence as a theory of punishment. A growing number of death row inmates (87 between 1976 and 2000) were released from death row after new evidence (often DNA evidence) suggested they might be innocent. In fact, there have been so many instances of improper proceedings at death penalty trials or of a failure to conduct DNA testing that the Governor of Illinois in the year 2000 called a moratorium on executions. Moratoriums were also under consideration in five other states ("Executions", 2000). What deterrent effect can a system have that is found to be unjust, capricious, racist? (See also Berns, 1979)

Not only does the United States have the highest percentage of its population in prison, but it also has higher crime rates than other western industrial nations (Chambliss, 1999). Throughout the 1990's, the rate of incarceration actually increased, even as the crime rate was dropping (Donziger, 1996). On the other hand, some nations are actually decreasing their imprisonment rates and substituting social policies without their increased leniency resulting in increasing crime rates (Pfeiffer, 1994).

At best, the results are inconclusive. Deterrent policies may or may not work, but, more importantly, the emphasis on deterrence may make us forget we have to be fair to the individual and not use him/her as a means to an end.

Another point involves the question of where does order in society come from? To promote the notion of deterrence is to make the rather Hobbesian assumption that it comes from the sovereign and must be imposed on bad people through force and fear. It is possible that the "get tough" Benthamistic deterrent approach to crime in the United States, exemplified by habitual offender laws and death penalty statutes, could easily throw aside respect for the individual, civil liberties and consideration of other solutions.

The central question remains. Is the prime issue crime control or justice for the individual accused of crime and justice for the society as a whole. If the prime issue is crime control, then one must be aware of the economic costs (police, prisons, criminal courts, locks on doors, CCTV cameras) as well as the political costs (loss of privacy). It may also be that one of the less analyzed costs may be attitudinal, that is, a loss of respect for individual human beings. This, in turn, may lead to even more crime.

Moreover, there seems to be a correlation between disparities in wealth in a nation and the emphasis on deterrence (Chambliss and Seidman, 1982). That is, the greater the gap between the rich and the poor, the greater the reliance on deterrence as the solution. Crime seems to occur when people feel they have no stake in maintaining the social structure, which may be why the crime rate is higher in capitalist nations as compared to socialist ones. The crime rate and punishment vary with levels of unemployment and strength of community bonds.

In conclusion, as we have seen in the 17th century, public floggings and executions led to riots and the politicization of the people and hence new methods of getting rid of troublemakers had to be devised. In England, the development of overseas colonies in America and Australia provided an opportunity to simultaneously get rid of troublemakers and provide free labor by transportation of criminals. Properly used, transportation could make it appear that the authorities were more merciful than hanging one's loved ones. But transportation provided only a temporary respite. With the closing of the colonies, the authorities were back to having to find some way of dealing with lawbreakers. The creation of the prison avoided the problems created by public punishments and provided the technocrats with the opportunity for experimentation in a new science of social control.

Thus, this chapter began with an analysis of some of the consequences of the nature approach to the study of man in the area of penal policies. If you recall from chapter one, the nature approach sees man as just another part of the deterministic universe which follows unavoidable cause and effect sequences. This simply denies the possibility of free will entirely. Man is just another part of the universe and he is caused to do all that he does by hidden but discoverable forces or mechanisms of nature. Man has no free will.

Presumably if one can discover these forces or mechanisms which make man behave as he does, one can use that knowledge to manipulate and control man who has thus been seen as a mere puppet on the strings of nature. We have seen how this approach is based on the faith in the absolute truth of science and how the possession of this truth is presumed to have liberated the social scientist from the bonds of determinism binding the rest of mankind. The social scientist has thus divided mankind into two classes of being, the puppets, all of whose doings are caused, and the scientists as the real knowers, who can and ought to control human dignity (behavior) and who presume their own benevolence in doing so.

We have seen from the beginning how these people, to varying degrees and with varying emphases, having achieved positions of wealth and power as a result of these developing natural sciences and technologies, had an unanalyzed faith in the science of molding others into their desired product. Thus, there was the attempt to utilize the newly developing technologies of the organization and control of people developing in both the military and factory systems of production to mold the inmates into the docile, hard working factory hand and law abiding member of society. Thus, we had the regimentation of punctual work schedules and solitary confinement combined with constant religious preachments and recriminations to convert the sinners from their sinful ways. The desired human end product was chosen by the authorities and not by the inmates. It was clearly a quest for a technology of controlling and molding people into desired end products whether the inmates wanted it or not. We thus have the tacit assumptions of the nature approach involving notions of the plasticity of man and techniques of molding him into a desired end product, without his consent.

There is also the unquestioned assumption of the right to do this on the part of the self-serving, self-righteous puppet masters. Questions of natural rights, liberty and the autonomy of individuals seemed to be issues of relevance for only the financially successful and the controllers of men.

On the other hand, there were others involved in the establishment of penal systems, who were primarily concerned with notions of reformation. Here, the nature approach did not apply. The convict was considered an erring child of God, someone who could with proper reflection and meditation, review his/her past sinful and criminal activities and resolve not to sin or offend again. In order to achieve this goal of reformation, solitary confinement was necessary. Tracts and printed sermons were distributed to the inmates and spiritual needs took precedence over any consideration of financial gain which might accrue to the state from the labor of inmates. Here, the individual was considered to have free will, which would enable him to choose a law abiding life upon release from prison. The convict was viewed as responsible for creating his own character and earning his eternal rewards. This was the spirit of the Pennsylvania model of penal policy.

Interestingly, Pentonville combines both of these strains of thought, the nature approach of molding inmates into desired end products and the nurture approach epitomized by the religious harangues daily delivered to inmates in the chapel. The contradiction between the approach of religious conversion dependent on the sinner deliberately choosing a new path and assuming responsibility for his actions as opposed to viewing man as a plastic puppet, a mere product of his environment to be molded as desired, seems to have been unnoticed or ignored by those in authority.

The attempt to mold inmates according to the visions of the controllers will be further explored in the next chapter on rehabilitation.

Chapter Three

The Doctor will Cure You—
Reflections on Rehabilitation

The term rehabilitation has been used in so many different ways that it is difficult to find a uniform agreed upon definition. At present, the word is used as a catch-all for extremely diverse policies ranging from religious conversion to the provision of educational and occupational opportunities in prisons to notions of behavior modification or pharmacological controls such as chemical castration. These diverse policies lumped under the heading of rehabilitation may actually be based on quite different and mutually contradictory conceptions of the nature of man, which find their roots in eighteenth century Enlightenment thought.

At that time, some believed that, since the truth of science seemed indisputable, it should not be suppressed by either the church or state. This led to notions of the autonomy of the individual, his right to use his mind, choose his religion, and to general notions of the rights of the individual which, as we have said, found expression in the French Declaration of the Rights of Man and the American Constitution. It might be noted that many of those who followed this approach still believed that normative standards could be found by the use of right reason. These normative standards and conceptions of right reason were very similar to those of Plato and Aristotle, and found expression in Thomas Aquinas' notions of natural law. This group, which might include such thinkers as Rene Descartes and John Locke, hoped that the objective methodologies of natural science would support and reaffirm the older ethical and moral standards and notions of human dignity.

However, for others, this new scientific epistemology, the notion that everything had to be reduced to measurable material cause leading to measurable material effect, contained within it the seeds of an absolute determinism and left no room for notions of free will or human autonomy. Such was the thinking of Thomas Hobbes and Jeremy Bentham.

Thus, we find for example, Hobbes' explanation of human "thought" as a material reaction produced in the brain by "sensations" (Hobbes,1651). His explanations of human sensations is reduced to the material motions or disturbances produced in the senses by the external world, which motions of the senses are transmitted to the brain by further material motions causing motions in the brain in a purely mechanical manner. Thought, therefore, is merely a material reaction. With such conceptions, notions of human autonomy and, indeed, of human dignity and liberty, simply disappear. Thus, man is reduced to a mere deterministic object to be studied and controlled, a product of the material forces or mechanisms of nature operating on him.

These diverse strains of thought stemming from the Enlightenment have resulted in two different political conceptions of modern man. The first strain emphasizing human autonomy and the rights of man, which are expressed in various governmental constitutions, including the American Constitution, are quite different from the deterministic model denying notions of autonomy and human rights and leading to a quest for scientific control of others.

While these two strains of thought have coexisted side by side to the present day, few people have recognized their incompatibility. What seems to have happened is that in some areas of life, we have paid attention to the first strain of thought and in other areas, we have paid attention to the second strain of thought.

Thus, when it comes to issues of constitutional law, democracy, and civil rights, we pay attention to the first strain. For example, modern conceptions of criminal law assume this voluntaristic model of man. First, it would be quite useless to make a law if people had no choice as to whether they would keep it or break it. It would be futile for me to command a stone not to fall since it cannot choose to obey or disobey. The very concept of law assumes free will in obeying or disobeying. The very idea of *mens rea*, necessary for guilt, assumes the deed was done deliberately. Our very notions of due process are based on our respect for the liberty and autonomy of the person accused of breaking the law.

However, those who accept the deterministic model of man, have no logical basis for considering and protecting the dignity, liberty and autonomy of the person. For example, it was his reductionistic image of man that led Bentham to reject the elaboration of rights and duties as the purpose of law and government. His rejection of notions of individual rights led to notions of the greatest good for the greatest number and social defense, which we have already critiqued.

Insufficient attention has been paid to the incompatibility and mutual contradictions inherent in these two approaches to the study of man, one based on notions of free will and human autonomy and the other based on determinism and the non existence of free will. Moreover, diverse policies based on these two mutually contradictory perspectives are commonly lumped together under the heading of rehabilitation. But such diverse policies should not have a common name.

Policies that assume the intelligence and free will of the individual in seeing the errors of his ways and choosing to be law abiding in the future are perhaps better termed reformation. These policies recognize that the individual is responsible for his choices. Thus, reformation would include policies of religious conversion, reintegration, and even such policies as the provision of education or job training programs, which are seen as merely providing the individual with an opportunity to earn a living in non-criminal ways. The ultimate decision of his way of life is up to him. These policies are compatible with the nurture approach.

On the other hand, policies which are based on a deterministic model of man (the nature approach), which deny man freedom of choice and view man as controlled by the forces of nature, whether biological, psychological or environmental, and hence in need of experts to analyze the cause and determine the cure of his criminality, are perhaps better termed rehabilitation.

Thus rehabilitation, as we have defined it, implies that criminal behavior is caused by some defect in the human puppet, which defect can be fixed by the expert who assumes the right to fix this defect whether the criminal wishes it or not. Puppets can not choose. The experts see themselves as merely benevolent menders.

Rehabilitation finds its expression in the various methods by which adherents of the nature approach have sought to explain human behavior. Approaches subsumed under the nature approach are: the biological approach, the psychological approach and the environmental approach, each of which has had its own process of development. We will examine each in turn.

THE BIOLOGICAL APPROACH

Prior to the 18th century, there was little conception of the idea of physical illnesses having different causes and requiring different treatments. The doctors tended to rely on vague explanations such as evil vapors or humors in the blood and to rely on traditional medicines or treatments such as blood letting, which were often ineffective and often did more harm than good. Hospitals tended to consist of large rooms filled with "sick" people, many of whom were infected by another's illness. (See Foucault, *The Birth of the Clinic*, 1973.)

By the 19th century, conceptions of scientific methodology, testing the truth of statements involving measurable cause and measurable effect sequences, achieved growing acceptance in the medical profession. This would eliminate ineffective medical procedures. The introduction of scientific methodology into the field of medicine led to the development of modern medicine.

By this time, the idea that different diseases should be studied separately, each having its own symptoms, etiology, prognosis and treatment, had developed. This led in turn to people suffering from different diseases being separated into individual wards of the hospital to enable each disease to be studied in isolation and uncontaged by patients suffering from other illnesses. It also led to doctor-surgeons seeking understanding of the workings of the human body through empirical methods. The only way to achieve this empirical knowledge was to dissect human cadavers.

Interestingly, the origin of the barber's pole goes back to this period in history. The people engaged in the medical-surgical field tended to be gentlemen-scientists who preferred not to get their own hands soiled by the blood and gore associated with surgery. The people who usually did the actual surgery under the watchful eye of the gentlemen-doctors were the barbers, who had sharpened tools at their disposal. Since bandages were used over and over again, the barbers merely washed out the soiled ones and hung them from a pole outside their establishments. The wind whipped the bandages around the pole and thus the origin of the red and white striped barber's pole.

Hogarth's painting, "The Reward of Cruelty," depicts this period of time in the history of medicine. (Pictured in, *Albion's Fatal Tree*, 1975.)

However, the general population was unwilling to accommodate the medical scientists' need for a supply of bodies for experimental dissection and demonstration to medical students. Hence bodies were in short supply. In desperation, the medical-scientists offered to pay for bodies, which promoted the practice of grave robbing by some unsavory ne'er-do-wells.

Imagine the horror and shock of those visiting a loved one's grave to place flowers or to pray, finding the grave dug open and the body of the loved one gone to what they considered the sacrilegious horrors of the dissecting room in the surgeons' hall. To these people, the surgeon-scientists appeared as unspeakable monsters engaging in foul practices, and they erected protective walls around cemeteries and placed watchmen in watch-towers to protect the graves. Mary Wollstonecraft Shelley's novel *Frankenstein* (1818) portrays the common person's view of the scientist-surgeon of this time. As graves became guarded, bodies became in ever shorter supply, so the medical surgeons in England petitioned the Parliament to add to capital punishment the provision that the bodies of the executed would be given to the surgeons for experimental and demonstration purposes. This resulted in further riots among the general population insofar as even the executed had loved ones who cared about them and were fearful that they would spend eternity in a dissected state (Linebaugh in Hay et al., 1975).

We have stated all of this as an historical context for analyzing the attitudes and definitions of these two groups toward each other. While the common people viewed the surgeon-scientist with horror and revulsion, these same surgeon-scientists viewed themselves as engaging in scientific progress and viewed the common people as ignorant obstructionists, referring to them as "Scum of the People." As Linebaugh has noted

> The formalized customs of bereavement, depending as they often did on the integrity of the corpse and the respect shown to it, were brutally violated by the practice of dissection. To the surgeons, their spokesmen and the lords and squires sitting in Parliament, not only was humiliation at the death of one of the "Scum of the People" a passing matter, but such further "Marks of Infamy" as public dissection became part of the policy of class discipline.
>
> (Linebaugh in Hay et al., 1975:117)

It is easy to see why this attitude paved the way for these surgeon-scientists to accept an image of the common people as being less than human.

Charles Darwin's publication of the *Origin of Species* in 1859 and his *Descent of Man* some ten years later, lent further support to the view that man was merely a product of nature and completely explainable in terms of forces or mechanisms of nature, the process of evolution.

Darwin's theory of evolution may be summarized as follows. He states that intergenerational small random genetic changes simply occur. For example, among birds born to the same parents, some may have bigger eyes or smaller eyes, some may have bigger feet or smaller feet. Once the genetic change has occurred, that change tends to be transmitted to future generations. Thus, the birds with slightly bigger eyes will tend to have offspring with slightly bigger eyes, ditto for the feet. A process of natural selection occurs insofar as these organisms are born into a pre-existing physical environment. In dim places, bigger eyed birds can see better and thus have a survival advantage. In bright places, for example, around cliffs on a seashore where there is no shade, smaller eyes have the advantage of cutting out glare. Eventually, this leads to birds living in dim areas all tending to have big eyes and birds living in bright places, all tending to have smaller eyes.

Darwin, unfortunately, referred to this as "survival of the fittest." However, on analysis, there is no absolute "fittest." Big eyes are not better than small eyes or vice versa. They are merely relatively adapted, small eyes for bright places, large eyes for dim places. This unfortunate phrase of "survival of the fittest" was to have grave consequences in legitimating the differential treatment and even the elimination of human groups perceived as biologically inferior.

All of these advances in the field of biological science occurred in the economic and social context of the 19th century, a period in which the development of commerce and industry had led to growing divisions between the rich and the poor. [See Hobsbawn, *Age of Capital*, (1975), and Thompson, *The Making of the English Working Class*, (1963).] The wealthier, industrialist classes were thus able to use some of these biological explanations to reaffirm their position in society, while rejecting any obligation to the less worthy, the poor and unfit. Social Darwinism had suggested that man, too, is subject to the forces of nature in a competitive struggle for survival. Some will survive (the fit), others will not be capable of the necessary adaptations and hence will not survive (the unfit). Therefore, the elimination of the unfit would enable society to progress and prosper. The doctrine of natural selection characterized human progress as a slow, natural, inevitable process of evolution, thus rejecting the notion of change by revolutionary means.

The poor were encouraged to accept their fate, nothing else could be done. Welfare legislation and any form of state care were opposed on the idea that competition for survival was an inevitable part of nature. Therefore, the "care and support of criminals, idiots, cripples and the like, merely prolongs human suffering, impedes human progress and contradicts the laws of nature" (Platt, 1969:20).

Thus, the new industrial and commercial classes, both in Europe and America, who had benefited greatly from the applications of technological and scientific ideas which reaffirmed their faith in science as the only way toward knowledge, considered the mass of workers and the poor merely as assets to be managed and troublemakers to be controlled. The children of the poor, as young as four years of age, were routinely used as labor in the cotton mills of New England, often comprising fifty percent of the labor force. As Tench Coxe, a champion of American industry has noted, the children were "the little fingers . . . of the gigantic automatons of labor saving machinery" (Quoted in Krisberg and Austin, 1978:13).

Since in the 19th century, biology was the field of progress in the natural sciences, the tendency was to seek the explanation of human doings and especially the doings of the criminal and troublesome classes as a product of their inferior biological makeup. It is often the case that the social sciences wish to put on the white coat of the natural sciences and use the latest theories and gadgets to seek the answers to social problems, the ontological differences between these two worlds merely denied away.

Thus, Cesare Lombroso, a professor of medicine and surgery at the University of Turin in the late 1800's, was greatly influenced by the thinking of Charles Darwin and Francis Galton (Lombroso-Ferrero (1911), 1972). Galton had been interested in the relationship of biological inheritance to personality and the utility of selective breeding policies for the elimination of undesirable personality traits.

In his work both as an army physician and prison doctor, Lombroso observed the phenomenon of tattooing among army recruits and criminals. He came to theorize that these marks were indications of a more primitive nature, given to violence which would have made early man more fitted for survival (Lombroso, 1896).

He began to engage in craniometrical measurements to see if he could determine a relationship between head shapes and types of criminality. He visited the jail in Naples to look at inmates' heads to see if they looked different from non-criminal Neopolitans and amazingly found that the inmates indeed were different. He assumed that their criminality was due to such differences and assumed that these inmates were atavisms, evolutionary throwbacks to an earlier stage of human evolution. Thus Lombroso described his criminal man.

The criminal by nature has a feeble cranial capacity, a heavy and developed jaw, a large orbital capacity, projecting superciliary ridges, an abnormal and asymmetrical cranium, a scanty beard or none, but abundant hair, projecting ears, frequently a crooked or flat nose. Criminals are subject to Daltonism; left-handedness is common; their muscular force is feeble. Alcoholic and epileptical degeneration exists in large number. Their nerve centers are frequently pigmented. They blush with difficulty. Their moral degeneracy corresponds with their physical, their criminal tendencies are manifested in infancy by onanism, cruelty, inclination to steal, excessive vanity, impulsive character. The criminal by nature is lazy, debauched, cowardly, not susceptible to remorse, without foresight; fond of tattooing. . . . In their associations they return to primitive social forms. The general cause of the persistence of an inferior race type is atavistic. Nature is responsible for the born criminal . . .

(Quoted in MacDonald, 1893:44–45)

However, many of the inmates were Sicilian migrant workers and clearly other factors such as cultural differences and differentials of wealth and power could more readily explain their incarceration, but this was unseen by Lombroso.

He was certain that an autopsy would prove his theory conclusively and when the most notorious of Italian criminals, Vilella, died, he obtained permission for the autopsy from the warden of the prison. Lombroso expected to find abnormalities in the brain, such that the brain of a criminal would resemble, not 19th century man, but the brain of a primitive species of man, thus proving that criminals were biologically determined to engage in crime and violence.

What Lombroso found was exactly what he was looking for, namely a distinct depression in the interior back of the skull, which he called, median occipital fossa, similar to that found in rodents. Lombroso was elated,

> At the sight of that skull, I seemed to see all of a sudden, lighted up as a vast plain under a flaming sky, the problem of the nature of the criminal- an atavistic being who reproduces in his person the ferocious instincts of primitive humanity and the inferior animals.
>
> (Quoted in Ferri,1900:12)

And while Vilella's brain did indicate some differences, they were not as extensive as Lombroso had expected to find. Nevertheless, Lombroso emphasized the differences in Vilella's brain, not the similarities to the brain of modern man.

And what should be society's response to the born criminal? According to Lombroso,

> As the born criminal is without remedy, he must be continually confined, and allowed no provisional liberty or mercy.
>
> (Quoted in MacDonald, 1893:45)

Lombroso's attempt to make his studies scientific indicates the general problem of seeking empirical causes for criminality. In his study of Sicilian inmates, he tended to find what he was looking for. More technically, it is an example of reliability (finding the same relationships consistently) versus validity (does one have the true explanation). Also, no degree of reliability can ever guarantee validity. With regard to his autopsy on Vilella, Lombroso was unaware that he was committing the *post hoc ergo propter hoc* fallacy. Just because one thing occurs before a second thing, does not mean that the first thing caused the second.

Cesare Lombroso and his graduate student, Enrico Ferri, elaborate the consequences of their biological determinist theory of criminality for the criminal justice system, which may be summarized and critiqued as follows:

1) If biology causes criminality, then the criminal in fact has no choice but to be a criminal. He cannot help his biology; he is not to be

blamed. He is not culpable, not guilty in the moral and legal senses. Here Lombroso's deterministic assumptions eliminate the very concept of guilt, and with it the corresponding moral and legal concept of innocence. The distinction between guilt and innocence simply ceases to exist.

2) Since he is not guilty, he should not be punished. Here, with the elimination of punishment as the purpose of the criminal justice system, the concept of retribution simply disappears, and with it the correlation between the gravity of the crime and the severity of the punishment. The seriousness of what one has done ceases to have a bearing on his sentence.

3) However, criminals should not be left free to wander in society and, must be taken into custody for the protection of society. It is not the deserts of the individual that is to be considered, so doing something to him is now legitimated in terms of social defense, a concept reminiscent of Jeremy Bentham's "greatest happiness for the greatest number" principle.

4) Since it is the biological experts who alone can detect the biological characteristics that cause criminality, they, not judges, should decide who is to be confined, under what conditions and for how long for the protection of society.

5) Since the protection of society legitimates the enforced confinement, clearly people must be kept confined until they are no longer dangerous, but they may be released as soon as considered fit to return to society by the medical experts, (not by judges). The period of custody is to be decided purely by the time taken to effect a cure, thus the period of confinement is to be indeterminate.

6) While in custody, they should be used to further develop the knowledge of biological causation of crime, in the same way as patients can be studied to learn more about their diseases. Additionally, such knowledge may enable the biological experts to identify future criminals even prior to their commission of crime and to confine them for the good of society.

7) Also, as medicine seeks to develop cures for diseases, so too we should use those in custody to seek cures for their criminality. If criminality is really only a biological problem, then the cure must be biological—medical or surgical.

8) Since the criminal is assumed to be devoid of free will, his permission is not to be sought. He is simply to be cured by the experts who presume their ability to effect a cure for the safety of society.

It is crucial to recognize at this point that all of these consequences for the criminal justice system logically flow from any deterministic theory of criminality regardless of the particular cause that is posited, whether this be biological, psychological or behavioral/environmental. We may be excused from responsibility for, and the consequences of, our actions only at the cost of delivering ourselves into the hands of the scientists-experts who will make all decisions concerning our fate.

The logic of Lombroso's position is entirely coherent given his initial assumptions of determinism. Additionally, it should be noted that the general assumption that criminality is a product of biology can never be disproved by empirical studies based on that assumption because of the plethora of biological characteristics available. If head shapes do not prove the link to criminality, then perhaps it is left handedness or red hair or genetic makeup. The possible biological causes of crime are extensive as the list below will indicate.

Within the field of biological determinism, crime has been explained by: head shapes (Gall-phrenology), body types (Sheldon), heredity (Dugdale's study of the Jukes), an extra Y chromosome (XYY theory), red hair, pre-menstrual tension (Dalton), post-partum depression, hormones, chemical imbalances, a low level of intelligence, or most recently in the United States in the mid 1990's, a defective gene found in African-Americans (The Violence Initiative) (Breggin and Breggin, 1994). This is merely a sampling of the various biological explanations held since the time of Lombroso. [See also, Williams (1991); Vold, Bernard & Snipes, (1998); Lanier and Henry, (1998) and Morrison, (1995)].

Most important are the consequences of these theoretical explanations for criminal justice policy making. Thus, if one believes that some aspect of biological determinism explains crime, one would support: medical-surgical solutions such as lobotomies, isolation for those deemed incurable by the medical experts, sterilization, compulsory drug therapy, or electric shock therapy among other solutions.

The treatment is prescribed by experts deemed to be capable of diagnosis of the cause of the criminality and expert in effecting a cure.

As noted earlier, the criminal or suspect is assumed devoid of free will and thus cannot object to this compulsory treatment, which may vary from expert to expert. The criminal is considered to be outside the judicial-legal process and thus is confined indefinitely until cured, even if this takes a lifetime. The criminal cannot refuse treatment, cannot appeal to legal authorities to stop the treatment, cannot opt for incarceration instead of treatment. His/her rights to autonomy and to access to the legal system have simply been taken away.

It should also be noted that biological theories have had wide ranging implications in the fields of politics and economics. The acceptance of biological theories in modern times is most obvious in Nazi racial theories, in which social Darwinistic notions of evolutionary progress through "survival of the fittest" culminated in the horrors of extermination camps. Interestingly, although Lombroso's notion of the "born criminal" had been largely discredited years before, E.A. Hooton, a physical anthropologist from Harvard University in the United States, set out to prove Lombroso was correct, which he believed that he did in the course of a well funded study. The time of his study was the 1930's—the era of Nazism (Morrison, 1995:129–130).

The assumption that women are victims of their hormonal conditions, such as pre-menstrual tension or post-partum depression, has been used to excuse individual women from responsibility for their criminal behavior; but this may also be used to exclude them from positions of power and influence and to justify paying women less than a man for equal work. The broader conception of some members of society being considered unfit has had ramifications in tax policies, education policies and social welfare policies as well as policies of segregation and apartheid.

Thus, for example, the work of H.H. Goddard and others (Vold, Bernard & Snipes, 1998) who claimed to show a link between intelligence and criminality was reiterated by William Shockley in America in the 1960's. Shockley, a Nobel physicist, believed that differences in IQ were related to genetic factors which, in turn, explained the differences in poverty and crime rates between black Americans and white Americans (Vold, Bernard & Snipes, 1998).

In 1994, the publication of *The Bell Curve* written by Richard Herrnstein and Charles Murray once again claimed that level of intelligence is the result of genetic factors and that low levels of intelligence are linked to crime and delinquency. Racial differences in IQ scores were attributed to biological factors.

Even though Herrnstein and Murray's findings have been highly criticized, those looking for biological explanations of crime and delinquency might indeed find their conclusions convincing. In America in the early 1900's, the Irish and later the Italians and others from Southern and Eastern Europe were identified as the inferior, criminal classes. The resulting policy was restrictions on immigration. Policies of sterilization were used against the feebleminded and the criminal, especially the feebleminded poor. Thus the American Supreme Court ruled in *Buck v. Bell* (1926)

> It is better for all the world, if instead of waiting to execute degenerate offspring for crime, or to let them starve for their imbecility, society can prevent those who are manifestly unfit from continuing their kind. The principle that sustains compulsory vaccination is broad enough to cover cutting the fallopian tubes.
>
> (Quoted in Williams, 1991:281)

What has been ignored in these policies are the American studies showing that IQ differences are more readily explained by language problems which tend to disappear after 20 years (Williams,1991:283).

Studies so far show that social factors and not genetic factors explain levels of intelligence and criminality. But as Williams has noted, racial explanations of criminality are particularly dangerous because,

> There seems to be a tendency to "prove" that the poorest groups in a society, especially if they are easily identified by ethnicity or color, are the most criminal and, according to some studies, the least intelligent. This might more plausibly suggest that criminality and intelligence have similar, environmental causes.
>
> (Williams, 1991:283)

THE PSYCHOLOGICAL APPROACH

While biological theories of criminality have not entirely disappeared, other explanations of criminality became more popular as we entered the early 1900's, namely, psychological determinism. It should be noted that psychological explanations of criminality share many of the same assumptions as biological theories. Psychiatrists are medical doctors, trained in the scientific method in their search for cause/effect relationships. In the area of criminal justice, they would use scientific methods to discover the cause and treatment for crime, feeling more comfortable in the nature approach to man rather than the nurture approach. One whose work has been used extensively in the field of criminal justice has been Sigmund Freud.

In 19th century Vienna, Sigmund Freud (1856–1939) was a product of his age, and a contemporary of Cesare Lombroso. Freud was imbued with a faith in science, such that he always spelled it with a capital letter S, believing science to be the solution to the world's ills. He studied medicine in Vienna, graduating in 1881. He was greatly influenced by his work with Ernst von Brucke in the area of animal physiology, and with the Viennese physician, Josef Breuer, whose research in the area of hysteria led him to conclude that hysterical cases can be treated while under hypnosis by bringing the causative idea out of the unconscious mind (Jones, 1961). His work with Jean Charcot, a French physiologist, convinced Freud that ideas can produce physical changes and that unconscious forces can influence people's thoughts and actions.

In brief, Freud believed that the personality contained three components, the id, ego and superego. Having defined the ego as existing on the conscious level, Freud diminished its importance and concentrated on the unconscious parts of the personality, namely the id and the superego. Freud believed that man's personality was a result of the battle between the unconscious forces of the id and the superego that produces complexes appropriate to each stage of development, especially the oral, anal and oedipal complexes, of which the adult is unaware. This explanation of personality and behavior as a product of these unconscious forces became the hallmark of Freudian therapists and forensic psychiatrists in the field of criminal justice.

Thus, even in the 1970's, the much publicized case of New Yorker George Adorno, who had killed many taxi drivers prior to robbing them, was explained as the acting out of an Oedipus complex. George was assumed to be a victim of a subconscious hatred of his father, whom he symbolically killed in the taxi drivers. In a sense, according to psychiatrists, George was as much a victim of his Oedipus complex as were the dead taxi drivers. George's rational explanation, when asked, was that he robbed the taxi drivers to get money and that the safest way to rob them was to shoot them first because dead men cannot resist and cannot identify you in court. The rationality of this explanation was rejected by the psychiatrists and dismissed as an unconscious defense mechanism to preserve George from the feelings of guilt that admitting a hatred of his father, whom he claimed to like, would induce. (Mc Eleney, J., 1970)

Note also the circular reasoning involved: George had an Oedipus complex because he killed taxi drivers and he killed taxi drivers because he had an Oedipus complex. The psychiatrist was convinced that he knew the answer because of his particular training. And, because of his professional credentials, his explanation was accepted by the credulous.

It is interesting to note that the explanation for criminal behavior that tends to be sought or given by a particular expert about a particular case usually flows from the expert's professional assumptions. In this case, because the expert was trained in Freudian psychology, the explanation came from the field of Freudian psychology. If the expert had been trained in biological explanations of crime, George Adorno's criminality might have been explained by his head shape.

Even experts in the field of psychology will often find different explanations for behavior depending on their particular branch of psychology.

In 1962, in the state of California, an anesthesiologist, suspicious that his wife of three months was unfaithful to him, brought acid home from the hospital in which he worked and poured it over his wife's body. Her screams were so loud that the doctor turned up the radio, for which he apologized to his neighbors, who eventually called the police. His wife died about a month later. The doctor had confessed to the crime, the neighbors had testified about her screams and the fact that he was present at the scene of the crime. Nonetheless, an insanity plea was entered, and what is interesting for our discussion is the different psychological explanations given by the experts in psychiatry/psychology who testified at his trial (Coleman, 1984:38–43).

All the experts testifying for the defense found the doctor to be insane at the time of the assault on his wife, but for different reasons. One psychiatrist claimed that this was a case of "multiple personality," an "alter ego" had committed the murder. But none of the other psychiatrists found evidence of this alter ego. A psychologist claimed the murder was the result of sexual problems, caused by a regression to an oral level of development and therefore the doctor was more interested in food, like any one year old child, than in sexual activity. The last psychiatrist to testify stated that the doctor was destined from early childhood to attack his wife because he was in fact a latent homosexual and was therefore symbolically killing his mother. He stated

> I don't think that at the deep levels of his personality, the doctor was really killing his wife. . . . This unconscious feeling, combined with the problem about his mother, swept this particular psychotic individual into a symptom which in his case was a criminal act-murder.
>
> (Cited in Coleman, 1984:41)

This case illustrates some of the difficulties with the scientific validity of psychological explanations of criminality. If scientific expertise truly exists, then should not there be uniformity in psychological explanations for criminal behavior?

Moreover, the jury in this case heard not only conflicting testimony from the experts for the defense, but they also heard testimony from the prosecuting attorney's psychiatric experts that the doctor was sane at the time of the crime. In fact, the jury rejected the claims of insanity by the experts for the defense and found the doctor guilty of first-degree murder.

This case also highlights some of the difficulties with one of the most public areas of psychiatry's involvement in the criminal justice arena, namely, the insanity defense.

In a legal sense, insanity has been used to refer to the situation in which the individual committing the crime "was unable to understand the wrongful or criminal nature of the act committed" (Coleman, 1984:47). This definition, gradually throughout the years, became broader, largely at the insistence of forensic psychiatrists, who in the 1960's in the United States developed what was popularly known as the "irresistible impulse" test.

> A person is not responsible for criminal conduct if at the time of such conduct as a result of mental disease or defect, he lacked substantial capacity either to appreciate the criminality (wrongfulness) of his conduct or to conform his conduct to the requirements of law.
>
> (American Law Institute, Model Penal Code, 1962)
>
> (Cited in Coleman, 1984:50.)

This definition of insanity, instead of clarifying issues of criminal insanity, largely made it more confusing for juries and judges. It opened the door to expert psychiatric testimony concerning the vast range of mental diseases, and whether or not the suspect had the capacity to understand his/her actions, and whether he/she had the capacity to willfully cause harm. Some even claimed that, if all behavior was a product of predetermined unconscious forces, as Freud stated, then all crime could be explained in terms of mental disease or defect.

As Menninger, author of *The Crime of Punishment*, (1968) has stated,

> The consistent use of a diagnostic clinic . . . would no doubt lead to a transformation of prisons, if not to their total disappearance in their present form and function.
>
> (Menninger, (1966) 1968: 251)

If the individual was found to be lacking in the capacity to understand the wrongfulness of his/her actions because of mental disease or defect, the individual was absolved of all responsibility for his/her actions and thus found "not guilty by reasons of insanity." No guilt, no responsibility, no punishment.

In fact, in some cases, the accused was found to have committed the crime while in a "dissociative state" such that the insanity lasted only seconds while the crime was being committed and the individual regained sanity "after he made the last stab wound" (Coleman,1984:51). For other examples, see also the Dan White case in California, or Sirhan Sirhan, the assassin of Robert Kennedy. (Coleman, 1984: chapters 3 and 4). The result is the same, not guilty by reason of insanity.

The person thus found "not guilty" would then be sent for medical psychiatric treatment and be eligible for release once the psychiatrists found the person cured of the conditions which had caused the crime. The length of time confined is left in the hands of the treatment experts, who may decide one is cured after a few weeks, a few months, a few years or never cured and thus in treatment for life. For example, Clara Gordon confessed to murder but was found to be insane at the time of her crime by two of the three psychiatrists who testified at her trial. She was sent to a psychiatric center for treatment, and was found to be no longer insane after only one week of treatment (Cited in Coleman, 1984:57).

On the other hand, Rennie cites the case of a New York inmate, transferred from Clinton Prison to Dannemora State Hospital for the Criminally Insane in New York State, who was confined for twenty-nine years, diagnosed as "paranoid" and "suspicious" because he alleged that the officials of the Clinton Prison were corrupt. The year was 1941. The inmate, Roy Schuster, filed numerous *habeas corpus* petitions, which were all dismissed. In 1963 a psychiatrist testified that the only symptom of his mental illness was his charge of corruption in the manner in which the prison officials had administered the New York State Department of Education Regent's Exam back in the 1940's. Despite the fact that in 1963 the court ordered a sanity hearing within sixty days, Schuster was still confined in 1975. The court, tired of waiting for the prison system to act, finally issued an unconditional release order on September 23, 1975. Had Schuster remained at Clinton Prison, he would have been eligible for parole in 1948 (Cited in Rennie, 1978:183).

Most recently, in the 1980's and 1990's in the United States, the insanity plea has undergone changes, largely due to the public's concern that criminals they believed to be guilty were found "not guilty by reason of insanity." This is perhaps best illustrated by the case of John Hinckley, who attempted the assassination of then President Ronald Reagan and who, despite what appeared to be careful planning of the shooting, was nonetheless found not guilty by reason of insanity because of his delusions regarding the actress Jodi Foster and his attempts to gain her attention by committing this offense (Coleman, 1984). Many American states have now adopted the plea, "guilty but insane," (a mix of punishment and treatment) or have eliminated the insanity plea altogether.

Thus, we have seen some of the consequences of psychological explanations for criminal behavior within the nature perspective. Crime is defined as a product of unconscious urges or forces over which the criminal had no control. As such, the criminal cannot be held accountable for his/her violation of law. He/she is, in effect, not responsible for the crime, and must be placed in the care of experts deigned to have the knowledge and expertise necessary to cure the criminal of the mental disease or defect which caused the crime. The course of treatment is left to the expert alone and it is important to note that this treatment may vary depending on the diagnosis of the expert and his/her particular training in the field of psychiatry.

Thus, individuals accused of the same criminal offense may undergo very different treatments and for varying lengths of time. The treatments may range from psychoanalysis, mandatory participation in counseling programs such as Alcoholics Anonymous or Narcotics Anonymous, to drug therapy, or even lobotomies and electric shock treatments. If treatment accompanies a prison sentence, the length of imprisonment is indeterminate, to be decided by parole boards operating on the advice of rehabilitative experts.

Because the individual was deemed not to have free will in the commission of the crime, he/she has no say in the treatment. "Among doctors, only psychiatrists may impose treatment on unwilling patients" Coleman, 1984:111).

As C.S. Lewis has stated,

> The things done to the criminal, even if they are called cures, will be just as compulsory as they were in the old days when we called them punishments.
>
> (Lewis, (1954)1970:288)

Thus, psychological determinism and its resulting policy of rehabilitation has been opposed on several grounds: for its lack of scientific rigor as in the statements of Vold and Cleckley, and for its denial of free will as in the statement of Lewis.

As Vold has noted,

> A methodology . . . under which only the patient knows the 'facts' of the case, and only the analyst understands the meaning of those 'facts' . . . does not lend itself to external third person, impersonal verification . . .
>
> (Vold, 1958:125)

And Cleckley has also noted that when he was teaching young physicians in psychiatric residency training, he found that the patients could be "led on in almost any direction" by the residents' line of questioning. Cleckley has stated that he became skeptical of the popular methods used to uncover what was in the unconscious and that the methods "cannot be counted upon as reliable methods of obtaining evidence" (Cleckley, as quoted in Vold, Bernard & Snipes, 1998:95).

Nevertheless, as Rennie has noted, "This is not to say that psychoanalysis is untrue, anymore than Goethe or Shakespeare are untrue, only that as a science, it presents great difficulties" (Rennie, 1978; 159).

In our view, the ramifications of psychoanalytic theory for the rights and autonomy of the individual are as significant and perhaps more so than the lack of scientific evidence to support this theory.

For example, in the former Soviet Union, dissidents were regularly defined as mentally ill and placed for "treatment" in psychiatric hospitals located in remote areas. The disease was described as "sluggish" or "creeping" schizophrenia, "the only symptom of which was the expression of politically unacceptable views" (Rich, 1991:13). Dissidents were treated with massive doses of psychoactive drugs, well isolated from public view. It seems obvious that dealing with political dissidents in this way, instead of accusing them of political crimes, which would have demanded a public trial and a forum for their political views, enabled the authorities to remove these individuals from society for long periods of time. They would be released only on the decision of the same psychiatrists who had diagnosed them as mentally ill in the first place.

Only recently (1991) have past abuses in Soviet Psychiatry been acknowledged with the admission that Pyotr Grigorenko, one of the founders of the human rights movement in the Soviet Union and a leading defender of fellow political dissidents, was confined unjustly in mental hospitals. (Rich, 1991) Grigorenko had been a former general in the Red Army and had received the Order of Lenin, the Soviet Union's highest award before he became involved in the human rights movement in the 1960's.

In the United States, psychiatry is being used in some states to confine criminal offenders beyond the length of sentence given to them by the courts. Thus, in 1994 the state of Kansas passed the Sexually Violent Predator Act. The act was designed to provide for the civil commitment of

> persons convicted or charged with a sexually violent offense and deemed to be suffering from a mental abnormality or personality disorder which makes the person likely to engage in the predatory act of sexual violence.
>
> (K.S.A. (1994) 59-29a01 et. seq.)

The act provided for a specific set of procedures requiring the court to find whether "probable cause" existed to support the finding that the person was a "sexually violent predator" and thus a future danger to oneself or others because unable to control one's behavior. After such finding, professional evaluation would occur and then a trial would be held to determine beyond a reasonable doubt whether the individual was a sexually violent predator. If that determination were confirmed, the person would be transferred to the custody of the Secretary of Social and Rehabilitation Services for

> control, care and treatment until such time as the person's mental abnormality or personality disorder has so changed that the person is safe to be at large.
>
> (K.S.A.(1994)59-29a07)

Persons so confined might be convicted violent sexual offenders who are eligible for release from prison, or persons charged with a sexually violent offense but found either incompetent to stand trial or "not guilty by reason of insanity."

The initial act provided for some constitutional safeguards for the person so committed involuntarily. Namely, the committing court had to review the case annually to see if detention was still warranted. The head (Secretary) of the Social and Rehabilitative Services Department, (which included general prison populations), could authorize the person to petition for release, but, even without the Secretary's permission, the individual could petition for release at any time.

The act was found unconstitutional by the Kansas State Supreme Court, but later upheld by a 1997 decision of the U.S. Supreme Court. (U.S. Supreme Court decision (1997) *Kansas v. Hendricks* No. 95-1649)

What is interesting for our discussion is the apparent confusion between notions of voluntarism and determinism, nature and nurture and punishment and treatment. The court states that this act is "a civil commitment scheme designed to protect the people from harm" (U.S. Supreme Court (1997) *Kansas v. Hendricks 95-1649.*) It applies only to those convicted of sexually violent predatory crimes (implying free will since found guilty after a public trial) or those judged "not guilty by reason of insanity" or "not guilty because incompetent to stand trial" (implying a lack of free will due to mental illness). The person so confined under this statute must be found to have a "mental abnormality" or "personality disorder." This determination was to be made by professionals in the field of psychiatry or psychology, a field, which rooted in the nature perspective, does not consider notions of free will, intelligence or rights.

Confinement may be for life, and may or may not entail treatment for the mental disorder, and yet the U.S. Supreme Court held that such commitment is not punitive since the aim is not retribution nor deterrence, but incapacitation or social defense.

ENVIRONMENTAL DETERMINISM/BEHAVIORISM

As early as the 1920's, Freudian psychology was being criticized as being untestable and unprovable. One either accepted it or one did not. As such, it was considered to be more like a religion than a science. This led to proposals that it was time to develop a more objective science of man based on quantifiable causes leading to quantifiable effects.

Pavlov's work on conditioning dogs to salivate at the sound of a bell was the first step in creating such an objective science insofar as the stimulus (the bell ringing) and the response (the dog salivating) were objectively verifiable.

It is simply unnecessary and, indeed, unscientific to discuss any untestable and unprovable intervening processes such as what the dog thought or expected. We can objectively say only that the bell is ringing and the dog is salivating. The stimulus (the cause) triggered the response (the effect). Additionally, the dog is conditioned to respond to the bell by a mechanical process of "association." One could devise experiments for how often, or according to what schedule, the dog had to be fed to the sound of a bell to make the association. In all of this the dog is considered as a purely passive object to be molded or remolded according to the wishes of the scientist.

Later research showed that, by feeding pigeons at one wall of a room, the initial random pecking behavior of pigeons could be modified into more locally concentrated pecking. Again, this process of behavior modification could be studied to find the most efficient modification methods.

These studies were deemed to have relevance to explaining the mechanisms of human "learning" and "behavior." If they had relevance only to training dogs and pigeons they would not have been given the universal publicity that they have.

Certainly, for B.F.Skinner (1972), all human learning and doing is assumed to be explainable as the product of randomly cast off behaviors which have been positively or negatively reinforced (strengthened or weakened) by, until now, unplanned "attractive" (pleasant) or "aversive" (unpleasant) stimuli from the environment. Accordingly, he views our world as an unplanned chaos replete with all the hurts and pains of life flowing from its unplanned chaotic nature. The solution is, of course, for the enlightened scientist, who understands all of this, to plan a better world and to utilize the "technology of operant behavior" to manipulate and control the masses into happily behaving as designed.

A technology of operant behavior is, as we shall see, already well advanced, and it may prove to be commensurate with our problems.
(Skinner, 1972:19)

That his solutions might not be in accord with notions of democracy and might be unacceptable to those obstructionists unwilling to deliver themselves and their futures into the hands of the omniscient and benevolent scientist is, for Skinner, simply an obstacle and an error to be disposed of. We really should not want to make our own decisions since, according to Skinner, we have no free will (autonomy), and what we think are our own decisions are really produced in us by operant conditioning anyhow, the only problem being that until now the "reinforcements" have been unplanned. It is time to abandon the notions of free will and all notions and practices based on it, including, we might clarify, notions of constitutional democracy and notions of human and civil rights.

We have moved forward by dispossessing autonomous man, but he has not departed gracefully. He is conducting a sort of rear-guard action in which, unfortunately, he can marshal formidable support. He is still an important figure in political science, law, religion, economics, anthropology, sociology, psychotherapy, philosophy, ethics, history, education, child care, linguistics, architecture, city planning and family life. These fields have their specialists and every specialist has a theory, and in almost every theory the autonomy of the individual is unquestioned. The inner man is not seriously threatened by data obtained through casual observation or from studies of the structure of behavior, and many of these fields deal only with groups of people, where statistical or actuarial data impose few restraints upon the individual. *The result is a tremendous weight of traditional "knowledge", which must be corrected or displaced by a scientific analysis.*

(Skinner, 1972:19) (emphasis added)

Likewise, he asserts we are to abandon notions of justice, deserts and principles of retribution in the area of criminal justice. A criminal is not to be punished but merely behaviorally modified by operant conditioning.

Another form of behavior modification was known as aversion therapy, the association of an undesirable behavior with an unpleasant or painful stimulation. This form of treatment for criminal offenders was the subject of a popular film by Stanley Kubrick, released in 1971, *A Clockwork Orange*. In the film, we are introduced to Alex, the leader of a violent gang who brutalize, terrorize and eventually kill. Alex is caught and sentenced to years in prison. When he hears of a new treatment which would "cure" him of his violent ways and, most important for Alex, release him from prison after only two weeks of successful treatment, he volunteers without knowing the exact nature of the cure. He is subjected to hours of watching violent films whilst being administered a drug which makes him feel nauseous and near death. Such is his "cure" that when released he is no longer able to defend himself and attempts suicide. In the film, because of public outcry, the therapists are forced to reverse the process.

In real life, aversion therapy and behavior modification techniques were widely used in the American penal system throughout the 1970's and 1980's. Wardens were encouraged to use the same brainwashing techniques on prisoners that had been used on American prisoners of war in Chinese camps and in Korea. Mail was withheld, mutual mistrust fostered; prisoner groups were disorganized with a system of spying and solitary confinement. To this list of techniques was added the use of drugs.

Behavior modification took the form of positive and negative reinforcements. This policy was used at Patuxent and other institutions in the penal system. Positive reinforcers would include: tokens which could be redeemed at the commissary for candy, apples, cigarettes; the step system which meant that you might be moved up from a dormitory sleeping arrangement to perhaps a four bed unit and ultimately perhaps a double or single room; home visits and days out. Negative reinforcers would be the withholding of these positive reinforcers, electric shock therapy, and Anectine suffocation treatments. It was believed that Anectine would be particularly effective since it was a poison derived from the South American arrow-tip poison, curare, which caused instant paralysis of all muscles, including those needed to breathe. At the brink of death, the therapist would recall the offender's wickedness, thus connecting the feeling of suffocation (dying) with the deviant behavior and inducing in the offender aversion from any such future deviant behavior (Cited in Rennie, 1978:182–3).

The Skinnerian approach wants us to abandon all of the insights and consequences for our living conditions gleaned from political science, law (especially constitutional democracy), religion, economics, anthropology (we would note especially cultural anthropology), sociology, psychology, history, and education. Can Skinner really be the only one who knows the answer? What do we lose when we follow him?

A very succinct critique of rehabilitation is offered by C.S. Lewis in an article he titled, "The Humanitarian Theory of Punishment" (1954). What is interesting is that at the end of the article he notes that he had to send this work to an Australian periodical since he "could get no hearing for it in England," such was the support for rehabilitation at that time (Lewis, Cited in Gerber and McAnany,1972:199).

Lewis begins by noting that, although the humanitarian theory (rehabilitation) appears mild and merciful in rejecting the harshness of retribution, this is a "dangerous illusion and disguises the possibility of cruelty and injustice without end." (Lewis, (1954) 1970:287)

> The Humanitarian theory removes from Punishment the concept of Desert. But the concept of Desert is the only connecting link between punishment and justice . . . when we cease to consider what the criminal deserves and consider only what will cure him or deter others, we have tacitly removed him from the sphere of justice altogether; instead of a person, a subject of rights, we now have a mere object, a patient, a "case."
>
> (Lewis, (1954) 1970: 288)

Lewis reminds us that the cure is compulsory and is imposed by technical experts "whose special sciences do not even employ such categories as rights and justice" (Lewis, (1954), 1970: 289). The criminal is detained until cured. Thus, definite sentences, which reflect some political consensus regarding proportionality between the crime and the punishment, are exchanged for indefinite sentences terminable only on the word of the expert. Thus indefinite sentences may actually result in a longer period of confinement than a definite sentence. Moreover, since crime and disease are considered to be synonymous, then the expert can call any state of mind he chooses a crime and compulsorily cure it. Lewis also notes the loss of liberty and the assault on the individual's personality which occur in mandatory psychotherapy.

> To be 'cured' against one's will and cured of states which we may not regard as disease is to be put on a level with those who have not yet reached the age of reason or those who never will; to be classed with infants, imbeciles, and domestic animals. But to be punished, however severely, because we have deserved it, because we 'ought to have known better,' is to be treated as a human person made in God's image.
>
> (Lewis, (1954), 1970: 292)

Chapter Four

It is All a Matter of Choice or Is It?
Reflections on Retribution

Retribution as a theory of punishment contains at least the following elements:

1. The offender is looked upon as having free will and, therefore, the commission of the offense was a free act (*mens rea* and *actus reus*). That is, the offender could have chosen not to commit the offense. The *mens rea* component refers to the notion that one must have done a legally prohibited deed deliberately. This concept is based on the notion of the autonomous nature of man — that we choose what we do. Indeed the very notion of having a legal system at all is dependent on having a voluntaristic conception of man. If man is deterministic, then he is controlled by nature and has no choice in what he does. It would be as senseless to forbid him to do something as it would be to command a stone not to fall. *Actus reus* refers to the fact that an unlawful act was actually carried out.
2. Since it was an act of will, the offender must be held responsible and therefore accountable for his/her actions. He/she has earned or merited the punishment (just deserts).
3. It is assumed that there is some societal agreement as to the definitions of punishable offenses and their proportionate punishments.
4. It is also assumed that the definitions of punishable offenses and their punishments are known by the people either by way of prescribed norms of behavior passed down orally from generation to generation or by a written set of codes.

5. The focus is on the punishable act, not the characteristics of the offender.
6. It is administered by the state under predefined rules.

The characterization of retribution as mere vengeance is a gross misrepresentation and misunderstanding, as we will attempt to show in the course of this chapter. Suffice it to say for now that retribution rejects malevolence, anger and hatred. The principle of retribution actually flows from a concern for fairness and a reluctance to punish. Its essence is that we have concern for the preservation of our own humanity and a serious recognition of the equal humanity of the offender. Retribution is actually a move away from vengeance.

Even its earliest formulation, the *lex talionis* (an eye for an eye and a tooth for a tooth), was intended to limit vengeance rather than as a slogan of malevolence. However, the concept of retribution has been much refined since then.

Neither should retribution theory be looked upon as a glib legitimation of policies which may be disproportionately harsh (habitual offender punishments) or which have little or no concern for the humanity of the offender. Such policies are, in effect, more akin to theories of social defense and deterrence, disguised as retribution.

Retribution theory is intrinsically connected to our image of man. What kind of thing are we? Do we think and decide, or are we mere puppets whose very thoughts and choices are a mere illusion, moved by forces and mechanisms of nature. This latter view has become the "coin of the realm," the currency of modern debate and the connector to all sorts of funding. But the "puppet" view of man is not compatible with a retributive theory of punishment.

The idea of responsibility for one's actions, which flows from notions of free will (voluntarism), has its roots in antiquity. We have only to look at ancient cultures and civilizations to confirm this idea. Thus Hoebel lists as Postulate VII of the Ashanti,

Men are endowed with conscious will, except when drunk or misdirected by an evil spirit in certain limited situations. (The corresponding corollary states) A man is morally, legally and individually responsible for his acts.

(Hoebel, 1976:253)

Thus, it is assumed that men and women have the intellectual capability to learn the norms (laws) of the society, to bring their behavior into conformity with these norms (laws), and to take responsibility for their actions when they disobey the norms (laws). To punish someone who is incapable of understanding the difference between what is right and what is wrong has always been considered unjust.

The beliefs, values and norms, having been taught to tribal members from childhood, form the basis for their system of law (Hoebel, 1976:26). Infractions were dealt with by way of individual or family responsibility. Criminal responsibility could extend even to some one who did not take part in the crime at all. Thus, for the Celts of ancient Ireland, "looking on" during the commission of a crime was a punishable act for which the offender had to pay a fine (*The Ancient Laws of Ireland*, 1865). More common is the notion that the clan or tribe is responsible for the actions of its members. This does not absolve the individual from criminal responsibility but merely extends the concept of responsibility to the offender's family, tribe or clan. This corporate responsibility was found among the Ashanti, Ifugao, Trobriand Islanders and others (Hoebel, 1976). Thus, if the offender could not pay the fine for his/her offense, the family or clan or tribe was required to do so (Hoebel, 1976 and *The Ancient Laws of Ireland*, 1865).

Collective responsibility for criminal acts disappeared almost entirely with the concept of individualism in the 18th century. Nevertheless, we sometimes hear verbalized this notion of collective responsibility when very young children commit heinous acts. That is, we as a society are all responsible when socialization into law-abiding behavior fails and crime results. Thus, the brutal murder of two year old James Bulger in Liverpool, England in 1994 by a nine year old and a ten year old elicited much soul searching as to how this heinous crime could have occurred. That is, how could society produce two such cold-blooded murderers, little more than children themselves? This concept of responsibility, whether collective or individual, implies that crime is a result of free choice or voluntarism (from the Latin word for will—*voluntas*). The members of the tribe or group are deemed to be capable of learning the law, of bringing their will into conformity with the law, and should be punished if they disobey the law.

In some tribal societies, the murderer takes on the added responsibility for his victim's family. This is true for the North American Inuit (Hoebel, 1976) and the Dinka of the Sudan. For the Dinka, this added responsibility takes on a new meaning since polygamy is practiced and the responsibility for caring for the victim's family means providing for the shelter, feeding, clothing and education of perhaps as many as 50 or 60 additional persons. No wonder that Dud Tongal, a Dinka, noted that the only murder he had heard tell of occurred when his grandfather was a young man (Tongal, 1975). For the Inuit, "a social principle requiring provision for the bereaved family places the responsibility directly upon the murderer" (Hoebel, 1976: 87).

This notion of responsibility has many dimensions in the criminal justice arena: the idea of individual responsibility for one's actions, the collective responsibility of the family or group for the behavior of its members, the responsibility of the offender not only for accepting the punishment imposed by the group but also perhaps for the care of his victim's family.

And, punishment (retribution) takes various forms. In primitive societies, one finds simple retaliation (blood feud), payment to the wronged party, penalties fixed by the tribe, banishment and death. Imprisonment was not used, because it was deemed necessary to keep the offender within the group, subject to the continuing moral and social influences of the group. In modern societies, one finds incarceration, death penalties, community service, supervision and fines. In both types of societies, the basic underlying assumption is that the individual is assumed to have the intelligence to differentiate between rightful and wrongful behavior and that he/she is capable of controlling one's behavior. If a crime occurred it was assumed that the offender could have prevented it. This notion of individual responsibility based on the intelligence and will of man is a theme common in all cultures and is reflected in philosophy, religion and literature.

The philosophical roots of retribution can be found in the writings of St. Thomas Aquinas, Immanuel Kant, and Georg Hegel.

For St. Thomas Aquinas, the intelligence and will of man is directed toward the good (Aquinas, (1273) 1947, vol. 1, QQ 78 and 87). Crime/sin is a misuse of man's will; that is, a talent designed to be directed to the good has been deliberately directed toward evil. Crime is therefore punishable, because man could have chosen the good (virtue) but chose evil (crime) instead. Crime is an expression of man's will and intelligence, a deliberate turning aside from the good, and hence punishable by both God and man.

Georg Hegel speaks of the act of punishment as righting a wrong committed by the will of man. The act of punishment negates the negation caused by man's deliberate act of willfulness against the common good. Hegel adds the notion that the criminal has the right to be punished, because in punishing we acknowledge his humanity, his will, his ability to choose (Knox, 1952). Or as Moberly has stated, reflecting on Hegel,

> . . . a criminal is honored by being punished, since punishment is an implicit tribute to his status as a responsible person.
>
> (Moberly, in Gerber and McAnany, 1972:76)

For Immanuel Kant, when an offender has violated the law, punishment is a categorical imperative.

> The law concerning punishment is a categorical imperative, and woe to him who creeps through the serpent-windings of Utilitarianism to discover some advantage that may discharge him from the Justice of Punishment, or even from the due measure of it, according to the Pharisaic maxim: "It is better that *one* man should die than that the whole people should perish." For if Justice and Righteousness perish, human life would no longer have any value in the world.
>
> (Kant, 1887:195–6)

Kant uses a parable to illustrate the necessity for punishment. He says, imagine that an island is to be destroyed tomorrow and there is one remaining murderer left on death row. What should be the community's response to that murderer? Let him go free, since he will be killed tomorrow anyway, or carry out the act of punishment. Kant states that the community must carry out the punishment, since in his view, not to punish for a crime committed would make of law-abiding citizens, accomplices in the crime of murder (Kant, 1887:198).

This notion of collective responsibility for punishment is found in primitive tribes as well. For example, as with murder of a Cheyenne by another Cheyenne, so for the Ashanti,

> criminal acts were those which were 'hated by the tribe'. More generally, they were hated by the ancestors. These were acts deemed to affect the relations of the community of Ashanti with . . . the ancestors of the entire tribe. Acts deemed offensive to the tribal ancestral spirits were held to affect the well-being of the tribe as a whole. Were they not to be

punished by the chief on behalf of the tribe, the ancestors would punish the entire tribe for its negligence and disregard of the natural law set by the supernatural ghosts of the departed.

(Hoebel, 1976:232)

This is similar to Kant's view that if the last remaining murderer is not put to death, even though the island will end on the morrow, all members of that community will be considered accomplices to the crime.

As Arthur and Marenin have pointed out, in traditional West African Ghana among the Ashanti,

swift and certain punishment was sometimes imposed by the extended family on its own members whose actions were adjudicated to have gone against the common weal. This form of collective punishment served to promote social stability while at the same time solidifying the collectively cherished sentiments and values held by the community.

(Arthur and Marenin, in Fields and Moore, 1996:166)

The notion that punishment represents collective values and sentiments is often lacking in modern society. Modern punishment systems are too often part of a political agenda to prove to the opposing political factions that one is "tough on crime" by way of harsher and more brutal punishments, which are nonetheless ineffective in either socializing offenders to law abidingness or in deterrence. Instead of keeping the offender within society and thus subject to the socializing influences that the Ashanti knew were important, we isolate the offender for extended periods of time, sometimes in complete isolation, expecting that in such dehumanizing conditions the offender will be deterred from future crime.

Implied in these philosophic notions of punishment is the idea of punishment righting a wrong (crime) and the collective responsibility for carrying out the punishment.

Retribution is a common theme in all religions, reflected in the concept of heaven as a reward for moral (law abiding) behavior and hell as punishment for immoral behavior. Unlike primitive tribes, in most religious belief systems (Islam, Judaism, Christianity), there is only the concept of individual responsibility. You go to heaven or hell on your own. The notion of collective responsibility is absent.

Islamic law and punishment provides a clear example of this concept of responsibility for one's actions and punishment for any transgressions.

When Westerners consider Islamic law and punishment, often the only thing that comes to mind is the harsh punishments: hand amputation for crimes of theft, one hundred lashes for crimes of adultery committed by persons not married, death by stoning for married adulterers, execution, crucifixion, amputation of hands and feet from opposite sides, or exile from the land for those who have committed the act of banditry or highway robbery and eighty lashes for the false accusation of a lack of chastity (Sanad, 1991). These are the punishments for *hadd* offenses, considered to be the most serious offenses in Islamic Law. They are deemed to be not only crimes but also sins, violating God's law as revealed to the prophet Mohammed in the 7th century CE. There is no separation of church and state. As Souryal notes, the legal system is based upon "prevention, conditioning, bonding, moralizing and punishment" (Souryal, 1988:23). Additionally, these offenses are considered serious because they endanger the basic structure of a community.

And Pope Pius XII has stated that the criminal has "consciously and deliberately violated a law which binds him" (Pius XII in Gerber and McAnany, 1972:61). Additionally, because every criminal offense is not only a violation of civil law but also a violation of God's law, the offender's attitude should be one

> . . . of acknowledgement of the evil done, (responsibility), . . . of aversion from, and repudiation of the evil deed itself, of repentance, expiation and purification, and purpose of future amendment.
> (Pope Pius XII, in Gerber and McAnany, 1972:63)

In order for the punishment to truly serve as a means of expiation and purification, it is necessary for the offender to suffer in order to achieve the interior purification necessary to return to the good. Thus, Pope Pius adds a moral dimension to punishment not usually acknowledged by civil authorities.

Interestingly, this moral concept of punishment finds expression in the character of the Reverend Dimmesdale in Nathaniel Hawthorne's, *The Scarlet Letter*. (1850,1959). The suffering noted by Pope Pius is not directly related to a public form of punishment imposed by the authorities, as was the case with Hester Prynne who was forced to wear the scarlet letter "A" as a punishment for her crime of adultery. Reverend Dimmesdale did not acknowledge his part in the offense and therefore was not publicly punished, but suffered nonetheless. He tells Hester,

> Happy are you, Hester, that wear the scarlet letter openly upon your bosom! Mine burns in secret! . . . the torment of seven years' cheat.
> (Hawthorne, (1850)1959:183)

His final purification comes with his public acknowledgement and responsibility for his sin/crime, and his repentance for the wrong committed seven years before.

Thus, as noted earlier, this concept of responsibility forms the basis for our modern system of punishment. Modern criminal law asserts that before there is a crime, there has to be both *actus reus* and *mens rea*. *Actus reus* means that something has been done which is explicitly prohibited by a criminal law. The *mens rea* component means that the deed was done deliberately. It looks upon the offender as having intelligence and free will. In other words, the offender could have chosen not to commit the offense.

During the period of the Divine Right of Kings, there was a tendency for the aristocracy, whose wealth, power and prestige rested on the maintenance of the status quo, to self-righteously appoint themselves as the discoverers and eliminators of the social evils which threatened their tranquility.

Many abuses arose from their tactics. People could be charged with offenses which were not unlawful when committed. They were denied knowledge of the charges or even the evidence against them until well into the trial proceedings. People were questioned in secret and were frequently tortured to confess all that they had done and to implicate others in the crimes at hand. Torture in questioning could be initiated on mere suspicion, such as the receipt of an anonymous accusatory letter. Spies reported on any statements critical of the King. No matter how rigorous one might be in upholding the law, one could not be certain of not being accused of a crime and taken into custody.

This arbitrary and harsh criminal justice system engendered a general disrespect for it among its subjects and, in fact, may have led to more crime on the basis of "you might as well be hanged for a sheep as a lamb."

Cesare Beccaria witnessed these injustices firsthand, and in 1764 wrote his *Essay on Crimes and Punishments*, which proposed a new criminal justice system, based on concern for individual human rights.

Beccaria, born in 1738, in Milan, a contemporary of Voltaire, Rousseau and Bentham, was a man of the Enlightenment, mathematician, economist, and jurist. His book of approximately 100 pages was translated almost immediately into twenty-two different languages (Pond 1999:15) and remains in print in the 21st century, more than two hundred and forty years later.

His work was influential with the revolutionaries who espoused two political revolutions, the American and the French, which represented freedom and autonomy for man against the oppression of dictatorial regimes. Thomas Jefferson, John Adams and other American revolutionaries cited Beccaria in their writings (Beirne, 1993).

Beccaria proposed first that there should be a written code of criminal law to protect citizens against the abuse of power by the state. This would guarantee that the state could not touch one unless one had broken a specific criminal law. This is our modern conception of *actus reus*. Also, there should be as few laws as possible so as not to restrict the liberties of the individual.

> . . . every member of society has a right to do any thing, that is not contrary to the laws, without fearing any other inconveniences. . . . (This is) a political dogma which should be defended by the laws, inculcated by the magistrates, and believed by the people; a sacred dogma without which there can be no lawful society. . . . By this principle our minds become free, active and vigorous; by this alone we are inspired with that virtue which knows no fear. . . .
>
> Attempts . . . against the life and liberty of a citizen, are crimes of the highest nature.
>
> (Beccaria, (1764) 1992:31)

Notice that we cannot simply punish things we dislike or find morally or aesthetically objectionable if there is no law against it, since this would violate the legal protections guaranteed an individual by a system of criminal laws. A law may subsequently be passed prohibiting these behaviors and subsequent violators may be punished according to law, but not until such a law has been passed.

Of course, Beccaria himself must be seen as a product of the social and intellectual transformations of his time: the faith in rationality flowing from the scientific revolution, a new power base of industry and commerce, and the rejection of legitimations of authority based on religion or royalty. The future of society was to be guided by human rationality rather than by revealed divine purpose. But this rationality was a rationality of men of a particular class in society—the new industrial, technological, scientific classes. Indeed, it could be argued that it was these interests, values and world views which were to direct the development of the new criminal law system. Their interests can be seen in such new notions as the transformation of the definition of private property into an absolute exclusive right,

> . . . that sole and despotic dominion which one man claims and exercises over the external things of the world, in total exclusion of the right of any other individual in the universe.
>
> (Blackstone, as cited in Hay et. al., 1975:19)

This radical redefinition of property devoid of notions of the common good or divine purpose creates an atomistic radical individualism with each individual concerned with the protection of his own individual rights and requiring the total predictability of a new legal system. In its development over time, this transduces into notions of legal positivism as found in the writings of Austin, Kelsen and others. "Law is the command of the sovereign," (Cited in Weinberg and Weinberg, 1980:10) or, as more commonly conceived, "we are a nation of laws, not of men" and the legal system itself takes on an idealized, independent reality.

For example, legal positivists arguing for retribution on a legalistic basis would claim that punishment is justified because the individual has decided to violate a law. According to these thinkers, it is the judge's responsibility to abide by and enforce the legal system and to give the legally designated punishment. It is not up to the judge to decide the rightness or morality of the laws concerned, nor is it within his authority to consider reformative or deterrent consequences. The judge merely applies the law as written. Thus Mabbott, in reflecting on his experiences as disciplinary officer of a college which mandated compulsory attendance at chapel, has noted that some students broke this rule on principle. He punished them not to reform them, nor to deter others, nor because he believed the infraction merited retribution, but because there was a rule and the rule had been deliberately broken.

> No punishment is morally retributive or reformative or deterrent. Any criminal punished for any one of these reasons is certainly unjustly punished. The only justification for punishing any man is that he has broken a law. . . .
>
> (Mabbott in Gerber and McAnany, 1972:44)

Mabbott is here following the general thinking of legal positivism that we are a nation of laws and not of men and it is not up to the individual to decide which laws he will obey and which laws he will not and that the law should be enforced simply because it is the law. This perspective gives reliability and predictability to a life governed by laws. It also guarantees the legal protections of the individual insofar as, if something is not explicitly prohibited by law, it is legally permitted and the state may not harm the individual by abuse of power. It also limits the state. These are powerful arguments in support of legal positivism.

However, it is conceivable that the legislator may enact laws on an *ad hoc* basis based on a particular political ideology or on notions of deterrence without sufficient regard for individual rights and the wider concerns of democracy. We have seen such a case in Nazi Germany as when the legally elected legislators made it a criminal offense to shelter members of the Jewish community who happened also to be citizens of Germany. Other laws resulted in the extermination of millions of Jews, Gypsies, and other groups targeted for extinction in the name of a racially pure state.

Some would argue that it is not sufficient for a law to have been passed procedurally correctly. For a law to be ethically enforceable requires that the law and its stated punishment must conform to other ethical or moral considerations.

Thus, Jerome Hall has noted,

> . . . the official "obligation" to apply punitive sanctions cannot be defended or even explained on the sole ground that "that is the law." It rests equally upon the ethical quality of the legal order which must be "basically just" . . . "the only justification for punishing any man" . . . is not "that he has broken a law" but that he has broken an ethically valid law . . .
>
> (Hall in Gerber and McAnany 1972:52)

Beccaria notes,

> That a punishment may not be an act of violence, of one, or of many against a private member of society, it should be public, immediate and necessary; the least possible in the case given; proportioned to the crime, and determined by the laws.
>
> (Beccaria (1764) 1992:99)

Beccaria proposed that punishments be specifically defined in the law and be proportionate to the seriousness of the offense. A serious crime would receive a grave punishment; a minor crime would receive a minor punishment. What is even more important, implied in this, is "no crime, no punishment." This protected the individual's liberty and immunity from the abuse of power by the state. This guaranteed that the individual would receive only the punishment he had earned and no more, whether or not that punishment deterred others. The protection of the rights of the criminal to a just punishment, we would repeat, was the sole consideration as required by notions of justice. Again we see Beccaria's concern for the liberty of the individual and protecting him from arbitrary and harsh punishments.

In order to further protect the rights of the individual, he proposed that:

1) a person should be considered innocent until proven guilty;
2) the accused had a right to know the charges and evidence against him;
3) the accused had the right to cross examine witnesses;
4) punishment should be swift and certain and carried out in public and
5) torture was condemned.

In addition, no one was exempt from the law. Punishment should be given to all who violated the law, whether at the bottom or the top of the social strata.

> The punishment of a nobleman should in no wise differ from that of the lowest member of society.
>
> (Beccaria, (1764) 1992:54)

In fact, he believed that the crimes of those at the top destroy the very ideas of "justice and duty" among the subjects (Beccaria, (1764) 1992:31).

Thus, Beccaria had proposed two separate arguments, one being the tenets of legal positivism and the other, notions of respect for the freedoms of the individual in society and the fair and just treatment of these individuals, requiring self constraints of the use of power by the authorities.

The very idea of having a system of criminal laws is, then, as concerned with the liberty of the individual and protecting him from the abuse of power by the state, even when convicted of a crime, as it is with merely prohibiting undesirable behaviors.

While Beccaria and Bentham are often linked in the classical school of criminology, they are really very dissimilar. Nowhere in Bentham is there expressed a concern for the rights of the individual. And nowhere in Beccaria is there the view of man as a mere puppet of nature. Beccaria's ideas led to The American Constitution (1789) and the French Declaration of the Rights of Man and the Citizen (1789). Bentham's ideas led to the Panopticon, CCTV cameras and control of man by the state.

Retribution, as a theory of punishment, is based on the theory of just deserts, that the criminal should be punished in proportion to the seriousness of the offense. It is based on notions of justice or fairness to the individual. This protects innocent individuals from any possible abuse of power by the state.

We would note from the outset that the requirement of justice to the individual is the absolute and exclusive rationale for punitive action by the state and it is a concept of justice, which is not found in either theories of deterrence or rehabilitation. As C.S. Lewis has noted,

> There is no sense in talking about a "just deterrent" or a "just cure."
> We demand of a deterrent not whether it is just but whether it will deter. We demand of a cure not whether it is just but whether it succeeds. Thus when we cease to consider what the criminal deserves and consider only what will cure him or deter others, we have tacitly removed him from the sphere of justice altogether; instead of a person, a subject of rights, we now have a mere object, a patient, a "case."
>
> (Lewis, (1954) 1970:288)

(See also, Radzinowicz, 1966:11–12.)

The principle of retribution, then, is concerned with protecting the liberties and rights even of a person who has been found guilty of a crime by limiting what the state may do to him. The concept of just deserts implies that we must be just even to the guilty. It assumes that we have a reluctance to punish. Its essence is that we have concern for the preservation of our own humanity and a serious recognition of the equal humanity of the offender.

This reading of retribution finds its expression in two concepts popular toward the end of the twentieth century. They are the concepts of "justice as fairness" and "restorative justice."

The Justice Model (Fogel, 1978) was an attempt in the late 1970's to re-examine the philosophy on which punishment systems and in particular, incarceration, were based. It was in large measure an attempt to deal with the criticisms leveled against programs of rehabilitation with their emphasis on the deterministic, "puppet" view of man. Those programs denied the concept of voluntarism or free will in both the commission of the crime and in the punishment. Criminals were assumed to have been caused to commit their crimes due to factors beyond their control, be they biological, psychological or environmental in nature. And because the individual was deemed to have no free will in the commission of the offense, strictly speaking, he/she could not be punished. Instead, he/she would be subject to rehabilitation by experts believed to be able to discern the cause of the criminal action and the corresponding cure.

These programs of rehabilitation were criticized, first on the basis of the denial of civil rights which resulted from forced treatment and secondly on the basis of a lack of evaluation as to success and cost effectiveness. The first criticisms emerged in Europe in the Nordic countries in the 1960's. As Inkeri Anttila had noted at that time,

> The criticism against treatment ideology has grown sharper. The parallel of the criminal-sick appears to be false. . . . This has led to an acute legal safeguards problem because of the absence of predictability and the absence of proportion between the seriousness of the crime and the strictness of treatment.
>
> (Anttila in Radzinowicz and Wolfgang, 1977:424)

In America, these criticisms were not publicly debated until the 1970's. Eventually however, decisions at the highest level of court review drew public attention to the denial of individual civil rights in involuntary treatment programs. For example, the case of *McNeil v. Director, 407 U.S.* 245 (1972) resulted in the immediate release of Edward

Lee McNeil from the Patuxent Institution for Defective Delinquents in the state of Maryland. McNeil, a twenty-five year old African American, convicted in 1966 of assault with intent to rape and assault on a police officer, was sent to Patuxent by the court for "evaluation and treatment" despite the absence of any evidence of insanity, drunkenness or drug addiction. The court's finding that he had a "limited tolerance for anxiety and stress" was based on his vehement denial that he had committed the offense (Prettyman in Fogel and Hudson, 1981:81). O'Neil was confined for six years at Patuxent without a hearing simply because he refused to participate in the evaluation process. Had McNeil been confined to a prison instead, he would have been eligible for release after a minimum sentence of one year and two months, or after a maximum sentence of five years. The Supreme Court of the United States ruled that his due process rights had been denied and that

an inmate who has not been adjudged a defective delinquent may not be held at Patuxent beyond the term of his original criminal sentence.
(Prettyman, in Fogel and Hudson, 1981:97, supra note 117)

Other court cases were instituted and other inmates soon released from Patuxent. Eventually, the facility was closed.

We have covered these criticisms of rehabilitation in a previous chapter, so suffice it to say that other criminologists soon added their concerns regarding the coercive nature of treatment under the guise of what was deemed a humane punishment/treatment system of rehabilitation. And these criticisms of rehabilitation soon led to a renewed interest in issues of free will and retribution, ultimately resulting in policy initiatives such as The Justice Model and restorative justice programs.

As David Fogel has noted,

Although free will may not exist perfectly, the criminal law is largely based upon its presumed vitality and forms the only basis for penal sanctions.
(Fogel and Hudson, 1981: viii)

The Justice Model was based on voluntarism or free will, the offender was assumed to have acted freely in the commission of the crime (*mens rea* and *actus reus*) and hence was responsible for his/her crime. Indeterminate sentences were replaced with definite, flat time sentences, parole was eliminated and offenders were to take charge of their own reformation by accepting or refusing educational, vocational or counseling programs.

The "citizenship model of corrections" was to replace what Conrad has referred to as "coerced rehabilitation" (Conrad in Fogel and Hudson, 1981:13). This citizenship model was based on the notion of rights and duties, rights owed to the offender by society, (the right to: personal safety, clean housing, adequate diet, personal dignity, work, self improvement, vote and a future). In return, the prisoners would be responsible for: contributing to a decent living environment within the prison, and treating other prisoners and correctional staff with dignity and in a respectful manner (Conrad, in Fogel and Hudson, 1981:18–19).

The justice model was based on retribution, in the tradition of Cesare Beccaria. As such it was non-utilitarian. Notions of deterrence, social defense or the forced treatments of rehabilitation had no place. In David Fogel's words,

> . . . punitive sanctions should be imposed on the offender simply for the sake of justice. Punishment is deserved; the form and severity of the punishment must, however, be proportionate to the criminal act. . . .
>
> (Fogel and Hudson, 1981:1)

This concern for justice was further exemplified by the focus in the 1980's on a restorative justice model of retribution. Although this model has various definitions, in general, restorative justice holds the offender accountable for his/her offense while recognizing that many injuries have resulted from the offense; injuries to the victim, the community and even to the offender. As such, victims, offenders and the community should be involved in the efforts to restore peace and harmony (Van Ness and Strong-Heetderks, 1997:31). The focus is not on vengeance, but reconciliation and reintegration of the offender to the community. As Moberly has noted, even though we might wish to inflict pain on the wrongdoer, our attitude should not be "unmitigatedly hostile."

> The wrongdoer had been our fellow citizen and he may be so again; basically he is friend and not enemy, and to recognize this must affect profoundly the way we are to treat him. The very same quality in him which makes it worth while to be indignant with him at all makes it wrong to allow indignation to monopolize our minds or even to dominate them.

Anyone who acts on an exclusively retributive principle is at fault.
(Moberly, in Gerber and McAnany,1972:75–76)

Thus the concept of restorative justice has resulted in various formats in which victim and offender can meet and pursue reparation and reconciliation. Victims have the opportunity to explain to the offender the trauma associated with the crime, the fear, the feeling of being violated, and the offender has the opportunity to explain his/her feelings to the victim. Often victims wish to know why they were the chosen target. Victim-Offender Reconciliation Programs, Family Group Conferencing and Victim-Offender Panels permit this exchange to take place. Often these programs allow for participation by others in the community (Van Ness and Strong-Heetderks, 1997:67–78).

Perhaps the most prominent of these victim-offender reconciliation programs has been South Africa's Truth and Reconciliation Commission, established by legislative fiat in 1995 to address the extensive killings, massacres and torture that had occurred prior to the end of apartheid. The Commission had the power to grant amnesty for these crimes, some of which had not been discovered previously. However, no crime of personal gain or malice would be eligible for amnesty. Often victims and offenders met face to face and the victims or their families could express their opposition to the granting of amnesty. If amnesty were denied, formal court proceedings could take place, but the decision to grant amnesty rested with the commission alone. Among fifteen other truth commissions around the world, only the South African commission had the power to grant amnesty. More than 21,000 South Africans, victims and witnesses, gave testimony to the Commission, of which 2,000 appeared in public hearings (Hayner, 2001).

That South Africans should seek healing in the context of a truth and reconciliation process should not be surprising. Concepts of restorative justice are rooted in ancient systems of tribal law. As E. Adamson Hoebel has noted in his study of primitive legal systems, the task of the law in these societies was

to clean the case up, to suppress or penalize the illegal behavior and to bring the relations of the disputants back into balance, so that life may resume its normal course.

(Hoebel, 1973:279)

Among the Ashanti and other African tribes prior to colonialism, imprisonment was unknown, and when the British introduced this idea, it was a matter of concern for tribal leaders since it was felt particularly harmful to isolate the offender from the influence of the tribe and tribal values.

> Usually punishments were administered collectively by the agents of social control, the offender's family, and the community at large in order to ensure that the offender did not become alienated from the community. . . . A punished offender had to be reintegrated into conforming society after the punishment was served.
>
> (Arthur, in Ebbe, 2000:253)

This concept of law can be seen in the ancient legal codes of: the Code of Hammurabi (1700 B.C.E.), the Summerian Code (2050 B.C.E.), the Code of Eshnunna (1700 B.C.E.), the Roman Law of the Twelve Tables (449 B.C.E.), the Lex Salica (496 C.E.), the Hebrew Scriptures (Van Ness et. al., 1997:8), the Brehon Law of Celtic Ireland (600 B.C.E.) and the Shari'a Law (622 C.E.), the basis of Muslim society even today.

In fact, in June of the year 2001, a murderer who was to be executed according to Shari'a Law was forgiven by the victim's father at the last moment when the executioner actually had his sword raised. The entire crowd rejoiced at the father's generosity and mercy, chanting "Allahu Akbar," (God is the Greatest), and the murderer knelt down and gave praise to God for the graces that had flowed at that moment (Wheeler, 2001). Everyone had risen above notions of vengeance or mere legal formalism. It is interesting that Shari'a permits this grace to flow.

Moments such as these make us pause to wonder about the relatedness of justice and mercy. Certainly the state was willing to uphold the law and only some one near and dear to the victim could forgive. No one in the crowd exhorted that the execution be completed. Perhaps everyone had grown more respectful of all life. Incidentally, according to the *United Nations Global Report on Crime and Justice* (Newman,1999), the lowest median reported rates for homicide among the nations of the world in 1994 were in Arab States and among Arab states, Saudi Arabia was reported to have the lowest rate of crime (Reichel, 1999:50).

This seeming reluctance to punish coupled with the idea that the offender should be reintegrated into the law-abiding community is found in primitive cultures as well as in modern nation states.

In America, the Native American Cheyenne's method of dealing with the murder of a Cheyenne by another Cheyenne, in their view the worst crime that could occur, seems to show also a reluctance to be vengeful. Since murder of the offender would only compound the offense, neither blood feud nor death decreed by the tribal council could be sanctioned. The murderer was banished from the tribe for a period of one to five years. If he survived, he could return to the tribe, but could not be chief and could not smoke the ceremonial peace pipe (Hoebel, 1976).

Another interesting facet of the Cheyenne's punishment/banishment ritual is the renewal of the medicine arrows, a ceremony at which all male members of the tribe had to be present. The Medicine Arrows had been with the tribe since time "beyond the memory of man" (Hoebel, 1976:156). When murder occurred, it was believed to cause a stain on the soul of the tribe and was revealed by the appearance of blood on the feathers of the Medicine Arrows. As Hoebel notes, the tribe as well as the murderer was stained. Purification was called for in the ritual of the Renewal of the Medicine Arrows. Absolute silence reigned while the Sacred Arrows were taken from their bundle and given fresh, unbloodied feathers. Thus, an event, which might have torn the tribe asunder and resulted in a vengeful treatment of the offender, became instead the means by which the solidarity of the tribe was confirmed and ratified. As Hoebel notes,

> So it was that the act which could shatter the unity of the tribe—homicide—was made the incident that formally reinforced the integrity of the people as a people. Not vengeance, nor further bloodletting, not the cruel punishment of imprisonment, but purification from a sin shared by all and a reinforcement of the social bond were the results achieved by the Cheyenne action.
>
> (Hoebel, 1976: 158)

The international criminologist Obi N. Ignatius Ebbe has noted that when a prison inmate is released from incarceration in Japan, community members greet him at the prison door and standing on either side of the door, clap their hands as they take him home in joy and jubilation (Ebbe, 2000:287). He is a member of the community whether inside the prison or outside.

This same concept is part of the penal philosophy of the Scandinavian countries. For example, in Denmark, incarceration is used sparingly, viewed as a "brutally negative" experience simply because it separates the offender from family and friends and leads "to the disintegration of social ties" (Henriques, in Ebbe, 2000:269). Thus, if incarcerated, the offender retains: his/her right to vote, to own private property, to plan his/her free time, receive money, and have the keys to his/her own room. Liberal leave policies are in effect after serving four weeks of one's sentence, and in some institutions inmates receive wages for work performed but are required to budget their funds to purchase food and other necessities. Thus, the values of individual responsibility are linked to notions of reintegration with the community (Henriques in Ebbe, 2000).

Ebbe speculates as to whether there is a direct correlation between low recidivism rates and humane treatment of incarcerated offenders stressing reintegration into the community after incarceration.

In the light of the foregoing considerations, let us consider current punishment practices in the United States. The United States has been incarcerating increasing percentages of its population and for longer periods of time. Mandatory and severe sentences have been written into the law at a time when other countries are moving away from such practices. Germany, for example, is moving towards a policy of decarceration with no ill effect on its crime rate (Pfeiffer, 1994).

Even in extradition treaties, foreign countries are required as a condition of extradition not to seek the death penalty. And yet the United States also has witnessed a great and well-publicized increase in executions. Almost nine hundred persons have been executed since 1972; ninety-eight were put to death in 1999, as compared to fourteen in 1991 (Bureau of Justice Statistics, (BJS), 2004). Despite criticism by the members of the European Union, Sweden, Australia, New Zealand and Japan regarding the execution of Timothy McVeigh in 2001 (the first federal execution since 1963) and the continuing use of the death penalty by the United States, President George Bush continues to defend the practice (Weinstein, 2003: A1).

One wonders why the United States is continuing to support these policies at such tremendous expense and inutility when other nations have rejected them. We have long known that prisons are colleges of crime. They alienate, they destroy families, they make it impossible for inmates to get back into the community. Once incarcerated, jobs are lost, housing is lost. Convicted sex offenders are reported to the local police, their names published. Can they fit in anywhere?

We believe we have shown in this chapter that the only rationale for punishment compatible with an adequate conception of man as an interpreter of reality, and hence with notions of democracy and justice, is the theory of retribution. It is also the only theory compatible with the legal protections of the individual from the possible abuse of power by the state. Certainly, punishment can only be fairly imposed on someone who has earned it, and fairness would require that the punishment not be greater than the seriousness of the offense.

But the question remains whether justice is an absolute value imposing obligations on the members of society to carry out the punishment in full, as Kant would have it, or whether other societal values must be taken into consideration. The punishment of the guilty individual often has serious consequences for innocent members of the community. It may lead to the breakup of families, the impoverishment of dependents, alienating even them from acquiescence in our justice system. The offender, despite Pope Pius XII's ideal of expiation and purification usually does not benefit from having been punished, certainly not from having been executed, and lengthy periods of imprisonment produce isolated, anomic and alienated, unhappy misfits. Should not a society concerned with the welfare of all its members seek to avoid these deleterious effects of Kantian punishments or mandatory sentences?

Perhaps some might argue that we must first punish and then reintegrate the individual into society, but this does not address the familial and societal effects of the punishment. For example, we discussed in chapter one the current imprisonment rates of African-Americans. (Over 30% of African-American males between the ages of 18–30 are in the control of the criminal justice system in the United States on any given day. In the city of Baltimore, Maryland, the figure is over 50%.) Certainly, to many African-Americans it would seem that our emphasis on legalistic punishment and our dismissal of other social policies, such as a system of national health care and an improved educational system, is misguided.

Moreover, it is a well known fact that African Americans are disproportionately arrested, convicted and incarcerated for crimes which if committed by white Americans would result in dismissal, fines or probation.

As we write, other nations, which have undergone civil wars and social upheavals, are trying to achieve the reintegration of their societies with instruments such as the South African Truth and Reconciliation Commission or the Good Friday Accord in Northern Ireland. In both examples, and there are others, both sides committed atrocities during a period when each side was fighting for what it considered its rights and considered members of the other side as sub-human enemies. To follow Kantian dictates now as they seek to integrate their society would re-engender familial and societal, passionate upheavals.

Chapter Five

Rewind and Fast Forward
Where Do We Go From Here?

Margaret Thatcher, a devout Christian, while Prime Minister of England, was asked what she considered to be the essence of Christianity. Her questioner, expecting her to say, "love" or "charity" was prepared to follow up with an attack on her economic policies which he viewed as lacking in love and charity, at least to those on the lower economic strata. He was not prepared for her answer, which was "Choice" (Humphrys, 2000). Though disappointed that she had not fallen into his trap, Mr. Humphrys notes that she was right of course, in that Christianity and indeed all religions present us with normative ideals and hold us responsible for our failures to live up to them.

Humphrys then proceeds to discuss voluntarism and determinism in human affairs in a manner which reflects popular current uncertainties about which view is the truth of our human condition. A common feature of the almost standard approach to this issue today is to cite the evidences of determinism, including our genetic inheritance and the human genome project and the influences of the environment ("environment" being quite a vague and ambiguous term, as we shall see.) The usual solution seems to be that the empirical evidence is against notions of voluntarism, but that, despite the evidence, we must cling to our faith in free will as a valuable illusion. But intellectual coherence requires that we must not even attempt to ignore the truth in order to accommodate delusions. The claim that man has free will is either factually true or it is factually false, and we must face the facts, however unpleasant.

This raises at least two distinct issues which need to be addressed separately, namely, 1) is free will a mere illusion and, if not, 2) why is this a valuable notion.

Is free will a mere illusion? Certainly those who became convinced that it is have already abandoned it as the foundation of their approach to their considerations of man and human affairs. Current doubts about the existence of free will are embedded in wider habits of modern thought which have had a long historical development. To understand the present, it may be necessary to re-travel the route by which we came and to re-examine some of the signposts along that route, paying special attention to notions of determinism influenced by developments of science.

The 17th century saw a rejection of theology and philosophy as ways of knowing and their replacement by the use of scientific methods (observation, mathematical analysis) as the only means of arriving at acceptable truth. Stephen Toulmin, in his *Cosmopolis* (1960), notes that the Thirty Years War (1631–1661), which was fought largely over conflicting religious viewpoints, had wreaked havoc all over Europe. Religious thinking seemed to provide no agreed upon answers nor social peace. People were looking for a new basis for consensus to avoid the conflicts over diverse religious conceptions.

For Toulmin, this search for a new basis for consensus led to the ready acceptance of the new epistemology of scientific methodology (Toulmin, 1960).

The condemnation of Galileo's teachings by the Vatican lent further support to the scientific community's rejection of philosophy and theology as ways of knowing. The decision was made that they should only talk about what they could "prove" by quantifiable measurements and mathematical analysis. After all, had not this method led to the new and revolutionary understanding of the heavens and the earth's place in it.

Especially after Newton's discovery of his laws of motion, scientific methodology seemed the only way to achieve the real, incontestable truth about anything. In essence, they believed that scientific truth was objective, absolute, and cumulative. It was objective in the sense that they thought that the facts spoke for themselves and an observer would simply see the truth. The truth, they assumed, was absolute in the sense that it was the answer once and for all. It was assumed to be cumulative in the sense that they believed the scientific method would pile truth upon truth to the explanation of everything.

Thus, it was decided that acceptable truth should be limited to what we can prove by measurement and mathematical analysis. The validity of Mathematics and Geometry was presumed to be indisputable because of their total internal logic.

> Mathematics represented all rational thinking which appeared necessarily true . . .
>
>   (Polanyi, (1958) 1962:9)

But this scientific epistemology necessitates a deterministic view of the universe in that the only explanations to be accepted are explanations of observable causes leading to observable effects unavoidably and regularly. Knowledge of these regular sequences reveals to us the real laws of nature.

Since this scientific method was the only way of finding the real truth about anything, this method had to be applied universally, that is, even to the study of man himself. As Karl Polanyi has noted, "from that time, (early 1700's), naturalism has haunted the sciences of man" (Polanyi, 1944:125–6). It has pervaded the study of man himself, conceived of as a mere object in nature devoid of free will, and his ideas or interpretations of reality being dismissed as mere epiphenomena, as we have already described in earlier chapters.

It has led to a quest for the mechanisms directing the processes and progress of society, as, for example, Comte's notions of the intellectual stages of history (the religious, the metaphysical, the scientific), or Marx's theory of the stages of economic development, or Spencerian social Darwinism (a notion which has had applications as diverse as justifying the holocaust perpetrated by the Nazis in Germany or legitimating laissez-faire economics), or Skinner's notions of positive and negative reinforcements, to mention but a few.

The epistemology embodied in scientific methodology eliminates the possibility of free will by fiat. Man has been merely presumed to be a deterministic being so that he may be studied by the methods of a deterministic science. They make man fit into their box instead of making the box to fit man. This itself is a metaphysical assumption that is unanalyzed.

Why man should fit into the box is never demonstrated. It is merely assumed that he must because of their faith that scientific "truth" was the only acceptable or consensus making truth and thus to say anything "true" about man, one had to arrive at that truth using scientific methodology with its deterministic implications.

That this raises the metaphysical question "what is truth" seems to have escaped their notice. But such a metaphysical question is simply beyond the scope of scientific methodology. As Burtt notes, those who proclaim the worthlessness of metaphysics can not thereby avoid metaphysical questions (Burtt, 1924). We shall return to this subject later in our discussion of the truth of science.

Perhaps Aristotle had held back the development of modern science by attributing human features to inanimate objects. Certainly, to say that a stone falls to be nearer to mother earth does not help us to develop the laws of motion. However, the social scientists have repeated that same mistake by trying to explain the actions and lives of humans by attributing to them the characteristics of the stone, thereby engaging in faulty metaphysics, and thus have held back the development of an adequate science of man. A science must be adequate to the kinds of things with which it deals. This point is eloquently made by E. A. Schumacher, in his *Guide for the Perplexed* (1977), in which he speaks of four different levels of being (mineral, vegetable, animal and human in ascending order), showing that each of the ascending orders has a defining characteristic that is not found in, nor explainable by, features of the lower orders.

> . . . modern thinking has become increasingly uncertain whether or not there is any "real" difference between animal and man. A great deal of study of the behavior of animals is being undertaken for the purpose of understanding the nature of man. This is analogous to studying physics with the hope of learning something about life. Naturally, since man . . . . contains the three lower Levels of Being, certain things can be elucidated by studying minerals, plants and animals—in fact, everything can be learned about him except that which makes him human.
>
> (Schumacher, 1977:20)

And such efforts are

> inane, like defining a dog as a barking plant or a running cabbage. Nothing is more conducive to the brutalization of the modern world than the launching, in the name of science, of wrongful and degrading definitions of man, such as the "naked ape."
>
> (Schumacher, 1977:21–22)

But let us return to the question of the nature of the truth given by science.

Recent work in the history and philosophy of science clearly shows us that the natural science enterprise is quite different from what that enterprise has traditionally been assumed to be. Thomas Kuhn, in his *The Structure of Scientific Revolutions* (1962), makes it quite clear that facts do not speak for themselves. He states that methodological directives are insufficient

> by themselves, to dictate a unique substantive conclusion to many sorts of scientific questions. Instructed to examine electrical or chemical phenomena, the man who is ignorant of these fields but who knows what it is to be scientific may legitimately reach any one of a number of incompatible conclusions.
>
> (Kuhn, (1962)1970:3–4)

Thus, empirical phenomena by themselves do not tell the observer the explanation. Indeed, the phenomena only make sense in the light of a humanly created explanation of them, and various explanations of the same phenomena are possible. It is the observer who creates and imposes the explanation on the phenomena. Indeed, to this very day there are no known forces or mechanisms of nature that can account for or explain this initial creation of meaning and its imposition on any given phenomenon. It is a creative act of the thinker and not a mere effect produced in him by some external mechanism.

Again, we might question the nature of the truth given to us by science. Kuhn makes it quite clear that science does not progress by the mere accretion of truth upon truth. He shows that scientific revolutions occur in which the explanatory "picture" (in the sense of "do you get the picture?") which ordered scientific "reality" is rejected and replaced by an altogether different explanatory "picture."

> Led by a new paradigm, scientists adopt new instruments and look in new places. Even more important, during revolutions, scientists see new and different things when looking with familiar instruments in places they have looked before. . . . Familiar objects are seen in a different light and are joined by unfamiliar ones as well. . . . We may want to say that after a revolution scientists are responding to a different world.
>
> (Kuhn, (1962)1970:111)

To summarize Kuhn, the process is something like the following: at a period which he characterizes as normal science, there is consensus about a particular explanatory picture and it is assumed that we know the explanations. However, over time, anomalies (phenomena which cannot be explained by the picture) occur. The scientific community tends to either ignore these phenomena or to fit them somehow into the accepted picture or paradigm. Over time, anomalies accumulate. Eventually, someone creates a brand new and different explanatory paradigm which explains both the anomalies and the phenomena explained by the older picture. This tends to be accepted by the younger scientists whose professional careers do not rest on the old paradigm. What now happens is a period of crisis in which scientists tend to talk past one another since they are speaking from different explanatory paradigms. Older scientists are not automatically convinced. The new picture becomes the new normal science over time as older scientists retire or die and the process starts anew (Kuhn, (1962)1970: chap. 7).

Thus, the truth of science, the explanation of empirical phenomena, totally changes. Science may be progressive, but it is not cumulative in the previously assumed manner of mere accretion.

In brief, science progresses by the rejection of older scientific explanations (truths) and replacing them with brand new explanations (truths) which explain even previously explained phenomena in an altogether different way. If this shows anything, it shows that even the scientific enterprise is only a human creation of meaning, an attempt to understand our world. It also shows that no deterministic mechanisms are involved in that human creation of meaning. Humans create explanations, they are not given in nature. The assumptions about the absolute indisputability and objectivity of the truth of science, which led to its exclusive claim to epistemological validity, simply do not hold up.

For example, it was known for thousands of years that the planets, alone of all the heavenly bodies, did not go around the earth as the perceived center of the universe in perfect circles. Yet, for the thousands of years, efforts were made to explain this event in terms of spheres rolling inside or outside spheres (epicycles) (See chapter one). The mechanical clocks based on this model still exist, which fairly accurately show the position of Mars among the stars through time. But facts do not speak for themselves. Hence the fact of the irregular pathways of Mars revealed no new explanation of the universe until Copernicus imagined looking at the universe from another perspective.

In his mind, he jumped on to the sun, an insane thought, and looked at the universe from there. Perhaps it was his readings of tales of the voyages of discovery, of different cultures and different (oriental) religions that influenced him to think of looking at the universe from a different perspective. But the astronomical data had been known for a thousand or more years and the data had told no one the answer. It took the burst of creativity of Copernicus which resulted in a brand new picture of the universe, and, all of a sudden, the universe became simpler mathematically. This is not the associationism of Pavlov, nor is it understood by positive and negative reinforcements, nor by some unconscious force of ids or superegos. A leap like this cannot be explained by any of these theories, nor by any Eysenckian amalgamation of them.

That human creativity is involved in the making of a new understanding is accepted by eminent members of the scientific community. As Michael Polanyi notes,

> What do we know about the process of scientific intuition?
>
> Surprising discoveries are often made on the grounds of observations that have been known for some time. Jeans quotes as examples the work of Copernicus, Galileo, Kepler, Newton, Lavoisier and Dalton, to which I would add Darwin's work, De Broglie's wave theory, Heisenberg's and Schrodinger's quantum-mechanics and Dirac's theory of the electron and positron. These inferences from known facts had to await the action of exceptional intuitive powers, and they clearly demonstrate the existence of such powers.
>
> (Polanyi, 1946: 13–14)

Science, then, is not that infallible enterprise that its early devotees believed it to be. It simply does not yield that objective, absolute, and cumulative by accretion truth, which they had assumed. Nor was it the simple application of scientific methodology (observation and mathematical analysis) which automatically yielded the truth. As we now recognize, even scientific truth is only a humanly created explanation (interpretation) of phenomena, a fallible effort of humans to make sense of their world. It is only *an* explanation, not *the* explanation. Yet it was these assumptions about the indisputability and objectivity of the truth presumably yielded by scientific methodology which had led to its facile acclamation as the exclusive way to find that "real" truth, which we now know simply does not exist. Scientists only interpret the phenomenon they examine and they are led to examine particular phenomena based on their interpretations. But this is precisely what the nurture approach to the study of man claims, that humans interpret reality. We create explanations of our world.

IS FREE WILL A VALUABLE NOTION?

Certainly, it would be unbearably depressing and fatalistically enervating to believe that, not only do our best laid plans *gang aft agley*, but that, in fact, our planning, our hopes, our laughter and our tears are really not even ours in the sense of our being the active agents therein, since we are merely passive and helpless dupes of a mere illusion. That very belief would render our whole experience of life and all of our efforts both futile and worthless.

But to consider that the only value of the belief in our free will is to avoid the intolerable recognition of our own passivity in the unfolding of our lives is to miss much of the importance and value of that belief in its manifold personal, social and intellectual ramifications.

It is a valuable notion because it rejects the idea of determinism and avoids all of its logical and practical consequences.

We have already considered some of the negative consequences of replacing the ontological conception of man as being an interpreter of reality, a creator of values and a chooser of consequences, with the opposite ontological conception of man as a deterministic passive product of forces and mechanisms of nature. We have already seen how this deterministic conception of man has logically and historically led to the displacement of considerations of the rights of the individual, of notions of justice, and even of conceptions of democracy itself and to their replacement by notions of social utility and a quest for technologies of control. Clearly, to those whose rights are not to be considered and who are to be controlled, this is an unacceptable political agenda.

An acceptance of the deterministic image of man logically results in the rejection from consideration of the many fields of thought and human endeavor based on conceptions of voluntarism and of all their practical implications. Skinner, as a determinist, is logically consistent but factually erroneous when he considers the fields of political science, law, religion, economics, philosophy, sociology, ethics, history, education, child care to be invalid and abandonable (Skinner,1972:19). To legitimate the creation of a redesigned society whose members are to be controlled by his "technology of operant behavior" he has to reject the entire field of human intellectual endeavor, the intellectual basis of democracy, law and justice. This massive rejection is based on his deterministic view of man as a puppet controlled by unsuspected controlling relations between behavior and the environment. But our purpose here is not to disprove Skinnner, we have earlier shown the roots of his assumptions. Our purpose is merely to show that the rejection of notions of free will would have massive ramifications in many areas of political and social life. With the deterministic image of man, we lose much.

Without notions of free will, political life as we know it would disappear. The very notion of democracy is founded on the ontological conception that all people are created equal in that they are interpreters of reality and deciders of what they want out of it and choosers of their desired consequences. A commitment to this view, especially on the part of those in power, is essential to their willingness to be voted out of power by elections.

But where any deterministic causal factor, or any amalgamation of such deterministic factors, is accepted by the leadership as the real explanation of the illusory wishes of the electorate, the basis for democracy and self-limitation is lost.

A clear example of this lack of self-limitation on the part of the political leader convinced of the correctness of his scientific understanding of man is Lenin's rejection of the opinions of the masses of workers and the imposition of his own will instead. As Spragens has noted,

> 'The vehicle of science', Lenin quoted Kautsky, 'is not the proletariat, but the bourgeois intelligentsia'. They are thereby entitled, indeed obligated, to engage in a 'fierce struggle against spontaneity', to 'divert the working class movement' from its own goals and 'bring it under the wing of revolutionary Social-Democracy.'
>
> (Quoted in Spragens 1981:147)

The constitution of the United States guarantees that such blatant tyranny cannot happen there, at least as long as the citizens maintain the intellectual foundations on which democracy is based, especially the conception of voluntaristic man. Yet, even in a democracy, an informed electorate should be aware of, and not be seduced by, the many techniques of manipulation developed by the empirical social sciences in the fields of advertising and the technologies of the manufacture of consumer desires or political consent.

Some of the early adherents to the faith in science as giving indisputable truth, which ran contrary to the views of the church and sovereigns, formed the arguments for the individual's right to think for himself. This in turn raised questions about the rights of the church or of the state to simply impose its thinking and its will on others.

Some of the early optimists of the scientific persuasion, such as Descartes and the early Locke, believed that science would put on an even more firm foundation the values and morals already accepted by them, but which actually flowed from the earlier conceptions of right reason (as opposed to mere rationality) embodied in the thinking of such as Plato, Aristotle, or the natural law theories of St. Thomas Aquinas. This earlier inherited tradition included a concept of man as an intelligent (reasonable) human being engaged in the human project of deciding how to achieve our human potentials as implied in the notions of the good man and the good society. Generally the notion of the good man involved notions of the considerate treatment of others and the restraint of mere self-interest and violent passions. However, their quest for an infallible philosophy based on scientific certainty excessively narrowed their vision and contributed to modern notions of determinism.

Another approach is reflected in Jeremy Bentham's philosophy of utilitarianism.

Bentham, because of his supposedly scientific reductionist image of man as a creature of nature merely balancing pleasure and pain, ends by ignoring considerations of individual rights, and hands all power over to a supposedly benevolent government which scientifically adjusts its laws and its policies for the greatest good of the greatest number.

In the preceding chapter, we have seen how the deterministic perspective consistently leads to denial of human responsibility and autonomy, which in turn leads to denial of notions of individual rights, which in turn leads to social defense, which becomes a political agenda with vague notions such as happiness or utility replacing notions of justice.

BUT WHAT IS GAINED FROM A BELIEF IN THE VOLUNTARISTIC IMAGE OF MAN?

Our belief in free will is more than a personally pleasant fiction anaesthetizing us from the unpleasant truth that we are in fact mere puppets. On the most fundamental level, our belief in free will affects how we see ourselves and each other. On a personal level, if I accept the concept of voluntarism, I must also recognize that I am responsible for my actions and for the development of my character through the practice of the virtues, all of which require a self-restraint and self-limitation, which do not come easily, especially at first. In brief, I must recognize that I alone achieve my humanity. This is a responsibility which is not to be taken lightly.

In interpersonal relations, this acknowledges the same characteristics in others and requires from them the same achievement of the virtues in the development of their own characters. It is only with the development of virtue that human relationships of friendship, loyalty and fairness are possible. Of what use am I to anybody as a friend, a spouse, or even as a parent, if my truthfulness, honesty and loyalty cannot be depended upon. If lack of character were common, life would, indeed, be lonely and unpleasant. Needless to say, the crime rate would also be high and we would seek to control crime by policies based on deterrence and social defense (hiring more police officers and filling more prisons).

Belief in the concept of free will would simultaneously recognize the autonomy of others and the recognition that we are engaged in the same struggle to achieve our humanity, which should engender in us both mutual sympathy and respect.

Man, though autonomous, is a social being. His sociality is not to be explained by biological pheromones, nor by some kind of herding instinct. His sociality is not that of an ant or a bee, nor is it some form of instinctive gregariousness that draws men together (Stark, 1976: vol.1).

Indeed, it may be said that man, though individually autonomous, is a social being for certainly we all live in societies but find ourselves in our particular niche in the myriad social relations of the society. On the general social structural level, these relationships include relationships of power and wealth, and on the more personal level, relationships of conflict or conviviality with our next door neighbor.

We are frail human beings who have to live our lives in the context of the social relations in which we have our place. This greatly affects the quality of our lives. We can live in peace and harmony or anarchy. This is a fact as much as any fact of physics.

But our sociality runs even deeper than this. If we recognize the fact that we are born with intelligence rather than with instinct, at birth we would have no knowledge of our world. Ernest Becker has noted that animals are protected by instincts given by nature, pre-programmed perceptions that call into play pre-programmed reactions. We have included this quote almost in its entirety, since to edit it would interrupt the flow of Becker's thought.

> It is very simple. Animals are not moved by what they cannot react to. They live in a tiny world, a sliver of reality, one neuro-chemical program that keeps them walking behind their nose and shuts out everything else. But look at man, the impossible creature! Here nature has thrown caution to the winds along with the programmed instincts. She created an animal who has no defense against full perception of the external world, an animal open only to experience. . . . He can relate not only to animals in his own species, but in some ways to all other species. He can contemplate not only what is edible for him, but everything that grows. He not only lives in this moment, but expands his inner self to yesterday, his curiosity to centuries ago, his fears to five billion years from now when the sun will cool, his hopes to an eternity from now. He lives not only on a tiny territory, not even on an entire planet, but in a galaxy, in a universe, and in dimensions beyond visible universes. It is appalling, the burden that man bears, the experiential burden . . . man can't even take his own body for granted as can other animals . . . Man's body is a problem to him that has to be explained. Not only his body is strange, but also its inner landscape, the memories and dreams. Man's very insides—his self—are foreign to him. He doesn't know who he is, why he was born, what he is doing on the planet, what he is supposed to do, what he can expect. His own existence is incomprehensible to him, a miracle just like the rest of creation, closer to him, right near his pounding heart, but for that reason all the more strange. Each thing is a problem, and man can shut out nothing.
>
> (Becker, 1973:50–51)

It is only by learning the cultural solutions created over time by our society that we are given a reality in which to be. Nevertheless, we do not absorb that reality merely mechanically like a tape recorder, but as active intelligent beings capable of reassessing and gradually re-creating that reality.

On the most general level of consideration, we can see that free will is an extremely important notion having vast implications; it is not a mere ostrich-like placebo. Faith in the concept of free will necessarily implies that each of us is involved in the human project of achieving a civilized and humane way of life, that in fact, we can create a barbarous and brutal or a gentler and kinder world, and that this potential implies a moral responsibility for the world we create.

The central issue, as we see it, is not doing more empirical studies to determine the mechanisms that work in producing human behavior or studying the efficiencies and effectiveness of criminal justice policies in reducing crime rates. The central issue is developing a more adequate picture of man.

The essence of our humanity is the fact that we have intelligence, that we are interpreters of reality and decide what things mean to us, and in doing so we create a reality in which to be. Our explanations of things resolve for us the terror and danger of the unknown and unpredictable. The Greeks understood this problem of the unpredictability, dangerousness and terror of the unknown, which they referred to as chaos. They saw the human problem of creating a cosmos, the understood, predictable and hence safe world. But, as Becker says, human questioning is not confined to an immediately present world of objects. We can look into the past and re-think it. We can look into the future and seek future goals. We can even look beyond death itself and wonder (Becker, 1973). Based on these understandings of our open ended reality, we decide what we want out of life, from wealth to sexual gratification to salvation.

Each of us is a living human being. Each of us experiences life with all its pains and pleasures, joys and tribulations on an intensely personal level. This is what Ortega y Gasset refers to as "radical personal reality" (Ortega y Gasset, (1957) 1963:39). I alone feel my toothache, I alone feel my hunger. No one else can feel it for me. It is only by my recognizing the "radical reality" of my life that I can understand and sympathize with yours. Yet Ortega y Gasset also notes that none of us chooses the time or the century or the society or his place in the social structure into which he is born. "Life," as he notes, "is fired at us point-blank" (Ortega y, Gasset (1957) 1963:42) and even tomorrow is an uncertain day in which we must make our way.

Each of us is born into a particular society in time and place, and each society has created its own interpretation of reality and corresponding social structure and human relations which create the context in which each of us experiences his "radical reality." Of course, each person's "radical reality" might make each of us concerned with only our selfish interests. My individual and personal experiences might lead me to consider only what benefits me.

Yet, as we have said earlier, man is a social being and from the earliest of times has lived in social groupings, from extended family kinship to the relations of modern societies. From the earliest of times we have had to find solutions to living together.

Some insights into the problem of establishing interactions with others is provided by Ortega y Gasset's discussion of the salutation, for example, the Western custom of shaking hands upon meeting one another (Ortega y Gasset (1957)1963: 197–202). We do not shake hands with family members and those we meet on a day to day basis, but we do perform the ritual when meeting those somewhat removed from us, acquaintances or strangers. Ortega y Gasset notes that no one forces us to do this and most people could not explain why we do it. Yet to refuse to shake hands would be considered an affront and put the other on guard. He speaks of this as a ritual which has lost its meaning but not its effect. The roots of the hand shake are lost in antiquity and explanations can only be guessed at.

Some say the proffering of one's empty hand to another showed that one was not holding a weapon and was thus a promise not to be dangerous to the other. Spencer interprets it as an act of submission, putting one's self in the hands of and at the mercy of the other (Ortega y Gasset, (1957) 1963: 199). Whichever its roots, it clearly shows a promise of trust in the non-dangerousness of each other, a promise which must be kept if the practice is to survive and human interactions occur. It clarifies that the meeting of another is fraught with dangerous uncertainties overcome by human promises.

Similarly, Bedouins, traveling in the desert approaching an on-coming caravan, dismount from their camels as they near each other, stop and have a brief meal in sight of each other, remount and dismount again at a distance of a couple of hundred yards, and walk past each other with the camels between them. This also is a promise not to be dangerous to each other. The practice may have arisen from the vulnerability of such caravans to pirates. Without the kept promises of non-dangerousness, human interactions would become impossible.

The very act of meeting someone is thus a promise to be trustworthy and not do the other person down (Lucas, 1980). This may be seen as merely the negative roots of ethical behavior. But clearly, as intelligent human beings, we have the potential to rise above merely not being dangerous to one another. Humans in their vast interpretations of the other and of our place and purpose in the cosmos create values or morals.

We can create notions of patience, truthfulness, generosity, kindness, loyalty. This is the only thing which makes each of us worthwhile as human beings and permits love, friendship, intimacy and companionship in life. The potential of achieving these things is both the promise and goal of our intelligence.

A society based on an adequate conception of man would reject punishment systems based on deterrence, or rehabilitation, or social defense. Theories of retribution rooted in legal positivism basically state that a person may receive only the punishment stated in the law. This may guarantee equality of treatment and the legal protections of the innocent, but in this age, with its emphasis on deterrence, the punishments set in the law itself, mandatory minimums or habitual offender punishments, (three felony convictions yielding a life sentence without parole), may be excessive and bear little relationship to the seriousness of the offense.

A just and fair system of punishment would recognize the equal humanity of the offender and have an empathy with his "radical reality," his existential day-to- day personal experience of life, recognizing that he/she is our fellow citizen and may be so again. Retribution theory should be based on a great reluctance to punish and not to do the offender "down," treating him/her as equal in all respects to me. It would also consider the harms done to the offender's family and community by the punishment of the offender. Of course, one must not ignore the victim and the harm done to victims by the criminal act. Someone must speak for the victim and the criminal should be held accountable and made to bear the consequences of his/her actions. That these punishments should not be excessive is clear in order to fulfill the most rudimentary conceptions of justice.

To specify the consequences in concrete form is a problematic puzzle. How many days, weeks, months, years in prison does an offender deserve? This indeed remains a puzzle. But what is clear is that the punishment system needs to be rooted in a cultural value system that is inclusive, guaranteeing to all equal access to life's opportunities and resources, where there is concern for the other person's experience of life, his/her "radical reality." Punishment systems would also be based on inclusivity, reintegration of the offender to the community of which he/she is a part.

Concepts of individualism, social Darwinism, and competition, rooted in a deterministic and rationalistic view of man, are not based on inclusivity but exclusivity, and hence cultures imbued with these values can never lead to the ideal of a true community of humans concerned for each other's well being, where all share in the resources of the society. Societies based on these concepts will be mired in crime and delinquency, a society of chaos, and no punishment system in the world will ameliorate this condition.

On the other hand, evidence abounds that societies which have the goal of inclusivity have low crime rates. Unless we begin to move in these directions, we will be stuck in the morass of the present. Perhaps these aspirations may be regarded as too idealistic, but it is equally true assuredly that the lower our aspirations, the less we achieve.

References

Ancel, M. (1972). New Social Defense. In R. Gerber & P. Mc Anany (Eds.) *Contemporary Punishment.* (pp. 132–139). Notre Dame: Notre Dame University Press.

Ancient Laws of Ireland. (1865). vols 1–5. Dublin: Alexander Thom.

Andenaes, J. (1966, 1972). General Prevention: A Broader View of Deterrence. In R. Gerber & P. McAnany (Eds.) *Contemporary Punishment* (pp. 108–119). Notre Dame: Notre Dame University Press.

Anttila, I. (1977) Conservative and Radical Criminal Policy in the Nordic Countries. In L. Radzinowicz & M. Wolfgang (Eds.).*Crime and Justice* vol.III, 2nd ed. (pp. 419–431). New York: Basic Books.

Aquinas, St. Thomas. (1273, 1947). vols. 1 and 2. *Summa Theologica.* New York: Benziger Brothers, Inc.

Arthur, J. (2000). Development of Penal Policy in Former British West Africa: Exploring the Colonial Dimension. In O.N.I. Ebbe (Ed.) (2000). *Comparative and International Criminal Justice Systems.* (pp. 251–265). 2nd Edition. Boston: Butterworth-Heinemann.

Arthur, J. & Marenin, O. (1996). British Colonialism and the Political Development of the Police in Ghana, West Africa. In C.B. Fields & R.H. Moore, Jr. (Eds.) (1996). *Comparative Criminal Justice.* (pp.163–180). Prospect Heights, Illinois: Waveland Press.

Beccaria, C. (1764, 1992). 2nd edition. *An Essay on Crimes and Punishments.* Boston: International Pocket Library.

Becker, E. (1973). *The Denial of Death.* New York: The Free Press.

Beirne, P. (1993). *Inventing Criminology.* Albany, New York: State University of New York Press.

Bentham, J. (1789, 1948). *The Principles of Morals and Legislation.* New York: Hafner Publishing Co.

Bentham, J. (1962). *The Works of Jeremy Bentham.* vol. IV New York.

Bentham, J. (1791, 1962) Panopticon in *The Works of Jeremy Bentham* vol. IV New York.

Berger, P. (1963). *Invitation to Sociology.* Garden City, NY: Anchor Books.

Berns, W. (1979*). For Capital Punishment.* New York: Basic Books.

Blackstone, W. (1769, 1906). *Commentaries on the Laws of England.* 3rd Edition. Albany, N.Y.: Banks and Company.

Boles, E. B. (1997, 2000). *Galileo's Commandment.* London: Abacus. A Div of Little Brown.

Breggin, M.D., P. & Breggin, G. R. (1994). *The War Against Children.* New York: St. Martin's Press.

Bronowski, J. & Mazlish, B. (1960). *The Western Intellectual Tradition.* New York: Harper Perennial.

Buck v. Bell. (1926). U. S. Supreme Court Decision. No. 292.

Budget OKs largest cell expansion in 70 years. (1998, January).Department of Correctional Services. *DOCS Today*, 6.

Bureau of Justice Statistics (BJS). (2003). Prisoners on death row by race. U.S. Department of Justice. Retrieved March 4, 2004, from http://www .ojp.usdoj.gov/bjs/glance/tables/exetab.htm.

Bureau of Justice Statistics (BJS). (2004). Executions. U.S. Department of Justice. Retrieved March 4, 2004, from http://www.ojp.usdoj.gov/bjs/ glance/tables/exetab.htm

Burtt, E.A. (1924). *The Metaphysical Foundations of Modern Physical Science.* London: Routledge and Kegan Paul Ltd.

Butterfield, F. (2004, April 30). Study Tracks Boom in Prisons and Notes Impact on Counties. *The New York Times*, p. A19.

Campbell,T. (1988). *Justice.* London: Macmillan Co.

Chambliss, W.(1999). *Power, Politics and Crime.* Boulder, Colorado: Westview Press.

Chambliss, W. & Seidman, R. (1982). *Law, Order and Power.* 2nd Edition. Reading, Massachusetts: Addison Wesley Publishing Co.

Christie, N. (1994). *Crime Control as Industry.* Second Edition London: Routledge.

Coleman, L. (1984). *The Reign of Error.* Boston: Beacon Press.

Conrad, J. (1981) Where There's Hope, There's Life. In D. Fogel & J. Hudson, (Eds.). *Justice as Fairness.* (pp. 3–21). Cincinnati: Anderson Publishing Co.

Descartes, R. (1911,1955) *Rules for the Direction of the Mind.* In (E. Haldane, & G.R.T. Ross, Trans.) *The Philosophical Works of Descartes.* Vol. 1. (1911, 1955). Dover Publications, Inc. (Original work published 1628).

Dickens, C. (1852, 1997). *David Copperfield.* New York: Penguin Books. Reprint Edition.

Donziger, S., (Ed.). (1996). *The Real War on Crime*. The Report of the National Criminal Justice Commission. New York: HarperCollins Publishers.

Duff, A. & Garland, D., (Eds.). (1994). *A Reader on Punishment*. Oxford: Oxford University Press.

Durkheim, E. (1933). *The Division of Labor in Society*. (G. Simpson, Trans.) New York: The Macmillan Company.

Durkheim, E. (1951). *Suicide: A Study in Sociology*. (G. Simpson, Trans.) Glencoe, Illinois: The Free Press.

Durkheim, E. (1953). *Sociology and Philosophy*. (D.F. Pocock, Trans.) Glencoe, Illinois: The Free Press.

Ebbe, O.N.I. (2000). The Unique and Comparative Features of the Criminal Justice Systems-Policing, Judiciary, and Corrections: A Synthesis. In O.N.I. Ebbe (Ed.). *Comparative and International Criminal Justice Systems*. 2nd Edition (pp. 277–289). Boston: Butterworth-Heinemann.

Ebbe, O. N. I. (Ed.) (2000). *Comparative and International Criminal Justice Systems*. 2nd Edition. Boston: Butterworth-Heinemann.

Elias, N. (1994). *The Civilizing Process*. Oxford: Basil Blackwell Ltd.

Esler, Gavin. (1997, 1998). *The United States of Anger*. London: Penguin Books.

Executions. (2000, June 10–16). *The Economist* (London, England), pp. 25–28.

Fellner, J.& Mauer, M. (1998, October). Losing the Vote: The Impact of Felony Disenfranchisement Laws in the United States. Human Rights Watch. The Sentencing Project. Updated by The Sentencing Project (May 2004). Retrieved June 7, 2004, from http://www.Sentencingproject.org

Ferri. E. (1900). *Criminal Sociology*. New York: D. Appleton.

Fields, C. & Moore, R., Jr. (Eds.) (1996). *Comparative Criminal Justice*. Prospect Heights, Illinois: Waveland Press, Inc.

Fogel, D. (1978). "... *We are the Living Proof* ... " *The Justice Model for Corrections*. Cincinnati: The W. H. Anderson Company.

Fogel, D. & Hudson, J. (Eds.) (1981). *Justice as Fairness*. Cincinnati: Anderson Publishing Co.

Foucault, M. (1973, 1975*). The Birth of the Clinic*. New York: Vintage Books.

Foucault, M. (1977*). Discipline and Punish*. London: Penguin Books

Garland, D. (1990*). Punishment and Modern Society*. Oxford: Clarendon Press.

Gerber, R. & McAnany, P. (Eds.) (1972) *Contemporary Punishment* Notre Dame: University of Notre Dame Press.

Giddens, A. (1991). *Introduction to Sociology*. New York: W.W. Norton & Co.

Goldworth, A. (Ed.) (1983). *The Collected Works of Jeremy Bentham* Oxford: Clarendon Press.

Haberman, C. (2000, January 9). Attica: Exorcising the Demons, Redeeming the Deaths. *The New York Times*, p. 7.

Haldane, E. & Ross, G.R.T. (1911, 1955). *The Philosophical Works of Descartes*. Dover Publications, Inc.

Hall, J. (1972) Just v. Unjust Law. In R. Gerber & P. Mc Anany (Eds.). *Contemporary Punishment*. (pp. 49–58). Notre Dame: Notre Dame University Press.

Hawking, S. (1988). *A Brief History of Time*. London: Guild Publishing.

Hawthorne, N. (1850, 1959). *The Scarlet Letter*. New York: Penguin Books USA Inc.

Hay, D.(1975). Property, Authority, and the Criminal Law. In D. Hay, P. Linebaugh, P. Rule, J., E.P. Thompson & C. Winslow (Eds.). *Albion's Fatal Tree*. (pp. 17–63). New York: Pantheon Books.

Hay, D., Linebaugh, P., Rule, J., Thompson, E.P., & Winslow, C. (1975) *Albion's Fatal Tree*. London: Penguin Books.

Hay, D. & Rogers, N. (1997). *Eighteenth century English Society*. Oxford: Oxford University Press.

Hayner, P. (2001). *Unspeakable Truths*. London: Routledge.

Henriques, Z. (2000). Treatment of Offenders in Denmark and Brazil. In O.I. Ebbe (Ed.) *Comparative And International Criminal Justice Systems*, 2nd. Edition, (pp. 267–274). Boston: Butterworth-Heinemann.

Herrnstein, R. & Murray, C. (1994*). The Bell Curve*. New York: The Free Press.

Hill, C. (1997*). Liberty Against the Law*. New York: Penguin Books.

Hobbes, T. (1651, 1960). *Leviathan*. Edited with an Introduction by M. Oakeshott. Oxford: Basil Blackwell.

Hobsbawn, E.J. (1975*). The Age of Capital*. New York: Scribner Publishers.

Hoebel, E. A. (1976*). The Law of Primitive Man*. New York: Atheneum.

Hudson, B. (1987*). Justice Through Punishment*. London: Macmillan Education Ltd.

Hudson, B. (1996, Reprint 1998). *Understanding Justice*. Buckingham, England: Open University Press.

Humphrys, J. (2000, July 2). We are bigger than our genes—thank God. *The Sunday Times*.(London). p. 17.

Ignatieff, M. (1978). *A Just Measure of Pain*. London: Penguin Books.

Jaki, S. L. (1979*). The Origin of Science and the Science of its Origin*. South Bend, Indiana: Regnery/Gateway, Inc.

Jaki, S.L. (1983). *Angels, Apes, & Men*. Peru, Illinois: Sherwood Sugden & Company, Publishers.

James, W. (1956). *The Will to Believe*. Dover Publications, Inc.

Jenkins, P. (1984). *Crime and Justice*. Pacific Grove, Calif.: Brooks/Cole Publishing Company.

John XXIII, Pope. (1961) *Mater et Magistra.* (W.J. Gibbons, S.J., Trans.) New York: Paulist Press.

John Paul II, Pope (1987) *Sollicitudo Rei Socialis.* (Translator not noted). Washington, D.C.: United States Catholic Conference.

Jones, E. (1961). *The Life and Work of Sigmund Freud.* New York: Basic Books.

Kansas v. Hendricks. (1997). U. S. Supreme Court Decision, No. 95-1649.

Kant, I. (1887). *The Philosophy of Law.* Edinburgh: T. & T. Clark.

Knox, T.M. (1952*). Hegel's Philosophy of Right.* Oxford: The Clarendon Press.

Krisberg, B. & Austin, J. (1978). *The Children of Ishmael.* Palo Alto, California: Mayfield Publishing Company.

Kubrick, S. (Director). (1971). *A Clockwork Orange.* [Motion picture].

Kuhn, T. S. (1962, 1970). *The Structure of Scientific Revolutions.* Chicago: The University of Chicago Press.

Lacey, N. (1988). *State Punishment.* London: Routledge.

Lanier, M. & Henry, S. (1998). *Essential Criminology.* Boulder, Colorado: Westview Press.

Lavin-Mc Eleney, B. (1985). *Correctional Reform in New York.* Lanham,Md: University Press of America.

Lenin, V. I. (1967). *Selected Works.* vol 1, New York: International Publishers.

Lewis, C.S. (1970) *God in the Dock.* Grand Rapids, Michigan: William B. Eerdmans Publishing Company.

Lewis, C.S. (1972). The Humanitarian Theory of Punishment. In R. Gerber & P. Mc Anany. (Eds.). *Contemporary Punishment.* (pp. 194–199.) Notre Dame: Notre Dame University Press.

Lewis, D.W. (1965). *From Newgate to Dannemora.* Ithaca: Cornell University Press.

Linebaugh, P. (1975). The Tyburn Riot Against the Surgeons. In D. Hay, P. Linebaugh, J. Rule, E.P. Thompson, C. Winslow (Eds.) *Albion's Fatal Tree.* (pp. 65-117). New York: Pantheon Books.

Locke, J. (1690, 1924). *Of Civil Government, Two Treatises.* London: J.M. Dent & Sons Ltd.

Lombroso, C. (1896, April). The Savage Art of Tattooing. *Popular Science Monthly*, (pp. 793–803).

Lombroso-Ferrero, G. (1911, 1972). *Criminal Man.* Montclair, N.J.: Patterson Smith.

Lucas, J.R. (1980*). On Justice.* Oxford: Clarendon Press.

Mabbott, J.D. (1972). Punishment as a Corollary of Rule-Breaking. In R. Gerber and P. Mc Anany. (Eds.) *Contemporary Punishment.* (pp. 41–48). Notre Dame: University of Notre Dame Press.

Mac Donald, A. (1893). *Abnormal Man*. Washington, D.C.: U.S. Government Printing Office.

Maguire, M., Morgan, R., & Reiner, R. (Eds.) (1994, 1997*). The Oxford Handbook of Criminology*. Oxford: Clarendon Press.

Matson, F. (1964). *The Broken Image*. New York: Braziller.

McEleney, J. (1970). Personal knowledge of case.

McNeil v. Director, Patuxent Institution (1972). U. S. Supreme Court Decision. No. 407 U.S. 245

Melossi, D. & Pavarini, M. (1981). *The Prison and the Factory*. London: The Macmillan Press.

Menninger, K. (1958). *Theory of Psychoanalytic Technique*. New York: Harper and Row.

Menninger, K. (1968). *The Crime of Punishment*. New York: Viking Press.

Moberly, W. (1972). Expiation. in R. Gerber and P. Mc Anany (Eds.) *Contemporary Punishment*. (pp.73–82) Notre Dame: University of Notre Dame Press.

Morrison, W. (1995). *Theoretical Criminology*. London: Cavendish Publishing Ltd.

Muncie, J. et. al., (Eds.). (1996). *Criminological Perspectives*. London: Sage Publications.

Murphy, J. (1995). *Punishment and Rehabilitation*. 3rd Edition. Belmont Calif: Wadsworth Publishing Company.

Newman, G. (1999). *Global Report on Crime and Justice*. New York: Oxford University Press, for the United Nations Office for Drug Control and Crime Prevention.

Novak, M. (1986). *Character and Crime*. Notre Dame: The Brownson Institute.

Ortega y Gasset, J. (1957). *Man and People*. New York: WW Norton & Company Inc.

Parekh, B. (Ed.) (1974). *Jeremy Bentham*. London: Frank Cass.

Pfeiffer, C. (1994). National Institute of Justice. *Christian Pfeiffer: Sentencing policy and Crime Rates in Reunified Germany* [Motion picture]. United States: Office of Justice Programs in the United States Department of Justice.

Pinker, S. (2002). *The Blank Slate*. New York: Penguin Books.

Pius XII, Pope. (1972). Crime and Punishment. In R. Gerber and P. Mc Anany (Eds.) *Contemporary Punishment* (pp.59–72). Notre Dame: University of Notre Dame Press.

Platt, A. M. (1969). *The Child Savers*. Chicago: University of Chicago Press.

Polanyi, K. (1944). *The Great Transformation*. New York: Rinehart.

Polanyi, M. (1946*). Science, Faith and Society*. Chicago: University of Chicago Press.

Polanyi, M. (1958). *The Study of Man.* Chicago: The University of Chicago Press.

Polanyi, M. (1958, 1962). *Personal Knowledge.* Chicago: The University of Chicago Press.

Pond, R. (1999). *Introduction to Criminology.* Winchester (England): Waterside Press.

Prettyman, E. B. (1981). The Indeterminate Sentence and the Right to Treatment. In D. Fogel & J. Hudson, *Justice as Fairness,* (pp. 69–99). Cincinnati: Anderson Publishing Co.

Radzinowicz, L. (1966). *Ideology and Crime.* New York: Columbia University Press.

Radzinowicz, L. & Wolfgang, M. (Eds.). (1971, 1977) *Crime and Justice.* vol. III, 2nd Edition. New York: Basic Books.

Randall, J. H. (1940). *The Making of the Modern Man.* New York: Houghton Mifflin.

Reichel, P.(1994, 1999). *Comparative Criminal Justice Systems.* 2nd Edition. Upper Saddle River, NJ: Prentice Hall.

Reiss, A. (1986). Reflections on Character and Crime. In M. Novak, *Character and Crime.* Postscript. Notre Dame: The Brownson Institute.

Rennie, Y. (1978). *The Search for Criminal Man.* Lexington, Mass.: Lexington Books.

Rich, V. (1991, November 16). Soviet Union admits to abuses of psychiatry. *New Scientist,* 132(1795), p. 13.

Rothman, D. (1971). *The Discovery of the Asylum.* Boston: Little Brown and Company.

Rothman. D. (1980). *Conscience and Convenience.* Boston: Little Brown and Company.

Ruggiero, V. et al. (Eds.) (1998). *The New European Criminology.* London: Routledge.

Ryan, A. (1993). *Justice.* London: Oxford University Press.

Sanad, N. (1991). *The Theory of Crime and Criminal Responsibility in Islamic Law: Shari'a.* Chicago: University of Illinois at Chicago, Office of International Criminal Justice.

Schopenhauer, A. (1893). *Studies in Pessimism.* London: Swan Sonnenschein & Co.

Schumacher, E.F. (1977). *A Guide for the Perplexed.* London: Jonathan Cape.

Sellin, T. (1980). *The Penalty of Death.* Beverly Hills, CA: Sage Publishers.

Sexually Violent Predator Act (1994). Kansas, United States. K.S.A. 59-29a01 et.seq.

Shapiro, I. (Ed.) (1994). *The Rule of Law.* New York: New York University Press.

Silving, H. (1972). The Dual Track System: Punishment and Prevention. In R. Gerber & P. Mc Anany. *Contemporary Punishment.* (pp. 140–148). Notre Dame: Notre Dame University Press, 1972, pp.140–148

Skinner, B.F. (1972). *Beyond Freedom and Dignity.* London: Jonathan Cape.

Solomon, R. & Murphy, M., (Eds.). (1990). *What is Justice.* New York: Oxford University Press.

Souryal, S. (1996). Juvenile Delinquency in the Cross-cultural Context: The Egyptian Experience. In C.B. Fields & R.H. Moore (Eds.) *Comparative Criminal Justice* (pp. 548–572). Prospect Heights, Illinois: Waveland Press.

Southport. (1999, September). *DOCS Today,* 10–13.

Spragens, Jr., T.A. (1981). *The Irony of Liberal Reason.* Chicago: The University of Chicago Press.

Stark, W. (1976, 1978, 1980). *The Social Bond.* Vols. I, II, and III. New York: Fordham University Press.

Strauss, L. (1936). *The Political Philosophy of Hobbes.* Oxford: The Clarendon Press.

System-wide SHU improvements underway. (1998, January). Department of Correctional Services. *DOCS Today,* 14.

Thomas, P. (1997, January 30). Study Suggests Black Male Prison Rate Impinges on Political Process. *The Washington Post,* p. A:03.

Thompson, E.P. (1963). *The Making of the English Working Class* New York: Vintage Books.

Thompson, E.P. (1975). *Whigs and Hunters: The Origin of the Black Act.* London: Penguin Books.

Tongal, D. (1975) Address given at Fordham University, Bronx, New York.

Tonnies, F. (1887, 1963). *Community and Society.* (C. P. Loomis, Trans.) New York: Harper&Row.

Toulmin, S. (1960). *The Philosophy of Science.* New York: Harper Torchbooks.

Van Ness, D. & Strong-Heetderks, K. (1997). *Restoring Justice.* Cincinnati: Anderson Publishing Co.

Vold, G. (1958). *Theoretical Criminology.* New York: Oxford University Press.

Vold, G., Bernard, T. & Snipes, J. (1998). *Theoretical Criminology.* 4th Edition. New York: Oxford University Press.

Walker, N. (1991). *Why Punish.* Oxford: Oxford University Press.

Weinberg, L. & Weinberg, J. (1980). *Law and Society: An Interdisciplinary Introduction.* Washington, D.C.: University Press of America, Inc.

Weinstein, H. (2003, January 12). The Nation: Move Will Intensify Debate on Executions. *Los Angeles Times.* p. A1.

Wheeler, J.(2001, June 27). *Last-minute reprieve from beheading*. Retrieved June 8, 2004, from http://news.bbc.co.uk/1/hi/world/middle_east/1410360.stm.

Williams, K. S. (1991). *Textbook on Criminology*, 3rd Edition. London: Blackstone Press Ltd.

Zimring, F. & Hawkins, G. (1973). *Deterrence*. Chicago: The University of Chicago Press.

Index